Good News, Bad News

GOOD NEWS, BAD NEWS

Journalism Ethics and the Public Interest

Jeremy Iggers

WestviewPress

A Division of HarperCollins*Publishers*

To Douglas Lewis,
with gratitude

Critical Studies in Communication and in the Cultural Industries

Published in 1998 in the United States of America by Westview Press, 5500 Central Avenue, Boulder,
Colorado 80301-2877, and in the United Kingdom by Westview Press, 12 Hid's Copse Road, Cumnor
Hill, Oxford OX2 9JJ

Library of Congress Cataloging-in-Publication Data
Iggers, Jeremy.
  Good news, bad news : journalism ethics and the public interest /
Jeremy Iggers.
      p.   cm. — (Critical studies in communication and in the
cultural industries)
   Includes bibliographical references and index.
   ISBN 0-8133-2951-5
   1. Journalistic ethics.   I. Title.   II. Series.
PN4756.I34   1998
174'.9097—dc21   97-48287
                                                                            CIP

The paper used in this publication meets the requirements of the American National Standard for
Permanence of Paper for Printed Library Materials Z39.48-1984.

10   9   8   7   6   5   4   3   2   1

Contents

A Richer Conception of Democracy, 148
Putting Pragmatist Values into Practice: Public
    Journalism as Journalism with the Public, 149
Increasing Civic Engagement, 151
What Role for Journalists? What Role for Experts? 152
The Disappearance of Public Space, 153
Beyond Newspapers, 155

Acknowledgments

I believe it was Mark Twain who said that he didn't care where he spent eternity, because he had "friends in both places." Having had the opportunity to work for newspapers while pursuing a doctorate in philosophy, I feel the same way. Without making the analogy too specific, I can say that this book would not have been possible without a lot of help and encouragement from friends in both places.

This book has its origins in my doctoral dissertation, written for the philosophy department at the University of Minnesota, and I am especially indebted to the members of my dissertation committee: Michael Root, Gene Mason, Charles Sugnet, Ted Glasser, and my advisor, Doug Lewis.

My own ideas about public journalism and the public responsibilities of journalists developed as a result of having the opportunity to put some of them into practice at the *Star Tribune* (Minneapolis–St.Paul). I have long believed that the best work in ethics comes out of dialogue, and when I wrote ethics columns for the *Star Tribune*, I was eager to find ways to engage readers in dialogue about the issues I explored.

The eventual result was a proposal to create Minnesota's Talking, a statewide network of public issues discussion groups. I am grateful to Linda Picone, former deputy managing editor, for supporting the proposal and giving it the resources it needed to become a reality. I also thank everyone else who contributed to its success: Liz McConnell, who edited the stories; Judy Atrubin, who capably managed the day-to-day operation of the project; and the many other colleagues who contributed time, effort, and expertise. The discussion materials and expertise provided by the Kettering Foundation and the Study Circles Resource Center were invaluable to the project and greatly enriched my own understanding of public deliberation.

My debt to Jay Rosen is profound. Having the opportunity to participate in the workshops of the Project on Public Life and the Press has broadened my intellectual horizons and enriched my understanding of the theory and practice of public journalism. My thanks, also, to Bob Steele, for the opportunity to participate in a Poynter Institute workshop on ethical decisionmaking.

I am also indebted to everyone who read and commented on the manuscript, gave advice, or simply offered moral support, including David Allen, Tom Atchison, Corinne Bedecarré, Eric Black, Kris Bunton, Art Charity, Bob Dardenne, Kathleen Fluegel, Bob Franklin, Steve Geimann, Hanno Hardt, Lou Hodges, Noel Holston, Bob Jensen, Maura Lerner, Liz McConnell, Ron Meador, Mike Meyers, Deb Monaghan, Peter Parisi, Linda Picone, Ron Salzberger, Jon Spayde, and Susan Wichmann. My thanks, also, to my editor, Cathy Pusateri, for all of her hard work.

Jeremy Iggers

Introduction

Janet Cooke's Redemption

In the spring of 1996, disgraced *Washington Post* reporter Janet Cooke resurfaced after years in obscurity. Banished from journalism in 1981 after her Pulitzer Prize–winning story of an eight-year-old inner-city drug addict was revealed as a hoax, Cooke appeared on ABC's *Nightline* with Ted Koppel and asked the American public for forgiveness and a second chance. Koppel heard her confession and then turned to the cameras for his closing summation:

> Some of you may wonder why what Janet Cooke did nearly sixteen years ago is still such a big deal to those of us in journalism. Many of you have such a low opinion of us anyway and are so convinced that we twist the facts, ignore the truth, make it up that you may think that we secretly revere Ms. Cooke as a role model.
>
> Lord knows that we have all collectively and individually contributed over the years to that sad impression of what we do. But there must be certain basic standards. What's wrong with American journalism today won't be drastically affected by whether or not Janet Cooke is rehired. What we should do is fire everyone in the business who is as deliberately careless of the truth today as she once was. (Ted Koppel, ABC's *Nightline*, May 10, 1996.)

It was a moment of great drama and solemnity. But is this really what is wrong with American journalism today? Are journalism's problems the fault of individuals within the news media who fail to live up to journalism's basic values? Can journalism's woes be cured by firing everyone who fails to live up to those standards? Or could the problem lie at least in part with the values themselves? Could it be that an increasingly irrelevant conversation within journalism about professional ethics distorts priorities and diverts the attention of both journalists and the public from the

1

more serious institutional failures of the news media to fulfill their responsibilities?

This book examines the role that journalism ethics play in shaping the direction and priorities of the press. The focus will primarily be on newspapers because it is in newspapers that the battle for American journalism's soul is still being fought.

This is not to suggest that what the reporters and producers at commercial radio and television stations produce is bad or unethical journalism. It is rather to suggest that, for the most part, what they produce isn't journalism at all. Robert MacNeil, former coanchor of the *MacNeil-Lehrer News Hour*, recently summarized the current state of television journalism by proclaiming "the end of news as we know it."

> By news as we know it I mean news produced by institutions practicing journalism, more or less observant of standard codes of good journalistic behavior . . . journalism treated if not as a learned profession at least as an honorable and respected craft with an important role to play in the democracy.
>
> I'm pessimistic . . . because all the trends in television journalism are toward the sensational, the hype, the hyperactive, the tabloid values to drive out the serious. In these trends, I see the end of news as a commodity of service to people and its conversion to an amusement, and I'm afraid that the values driving news in that direction will only increase with competition.[1]

Network television news has become, in the words of another observer, "a world of UFOs, psychics, daydreams, miracle cures, cuddly animals, O. J. Simpson, JonBenet Ramsey and, from time to time—at least for a few minutes—real news."[2] In other words, it has become a lot like local news, except that local news may place a higher premium on dramatic scenes of violence. There is little pretense of providing an accurate and comprehensive account of the day's news. The routine operations of local government are almost completely ignored, and when major political events and issues are covered, it is usually without the context that would make them meaningful. Public radio at the national level still produces journalism of a high standard, but its quality and impact at the local level varies with the strength of its local affiliates.

Journalism may be faring better in newspapers than in television, but the difference is only one of degree. Less and less of the content of newspapers is actually news in the traditional sense—information of importance to readers as citizens and members of communities—while an increasing proportion is given over to lifestyle features and information of interest to readers as consumers—stories about health care, entertainment, or other goods and services.

This much is certain: these are troubled times for American journalism. Publicly held newspaper companies that have traditionally produced an annual return on investment of 20 to 40 percent are under pressure from investors to continue to produce very high profits in spite of greatly increased competition for advertising dollars, fluctuating costs of newsprint, and static or declining readership. This has resulted in tightened budgets, shrinking news holes, and pressure to explore new sources of revenue that sometimes challenge the ethical boundaries of the newsroom.

Newsrooms have also experienced a loss of autonomy as locally owned news operations have been acquired by national chains. The impact of chain ownership on newspapers is debatable; in some cases, the quality of journalism may have improved, but in general, the most notable impact seems to be an increased emphasis on the bottom line. At the same time, television networks have been bought up by larger corporate conglomerates for which journalism is only a subsidiary enterprise.

Inside the profession, discontent mounts. There is a pervasive sense in newsrooms that journalism's best days are over. Real income for most journalists has declined sharply over the past decade, and the intrinsic satisfactions that once compensated for a lower income have diminished as the newsroom environment has been increasingly corporatized. Hard news has been forced to retreat as more and more column space is given over to lifestyle features. "Working for a newspaper used to seem like a noble and exciting calling," concludes Carl Sessions Stepp in the *American Journalism Review*. "Now the business side has triumphed and angst reigns in America's newsrooms."[3]

At the same time, news operations face a loss of audience. According to the Pew Research Center for the People and the Press, viewership of network news programs on CBS, ABC, and NBC declined from 60 percent in 1993 to 48 percent in 1996. Some of that audience has doubtless switched to other news options such as CNN and CNBC, but a comparison of viewership statistics from the 1992 and 1996 elections suggests that the overall audience for news programming has declined. Newspaper readership has suffered a similar decline; according to a 1995 study by the Times Mirror Center for the People and the Press, 45 percent of Americans surveyed in March of that year said they had read a newspaper the previous day, compared with 58 percent in 1994 and 71 percent in 1965.[4] A growing number of Americans have, it seems, simply stopped following the news.

The dailies no longer hold the central place they once held in public life, and many forecasters predict a further decline into irrelevance as the average age of newspaper readers rises and younger information-seekers turn to technologies such as the Internet. A 1996 study predicts that newspaper readership, already in sharp decline, will have lost as much as 14 percent to the Internet between 1996 and the year 2001.[5]

The loss of audience has been accompanied by—and perhaps partly caused by—a loss of credibility and respect. Seventy-one percent of respondents to a 1994 *Times Mirror* survey felt that the media "stand in the way of America solving its problems." By 1996, that figure had improved to 54 percent, still hardly a vote of confidence.[6]

Moreover, newspapers are experiencing the fallout of a larger crisis in the culture, a period of cultural upheaval that is sometimes described as the end of the modern era. There is a growing acceptance of the idea that reality is socially constructed and that the competing versions of reality presented to us via the news media are not and indeed cannot be unbiased representations of reality. Faith in facts has given way to an understanding that facts don't interpret themselves and to a distrust of all sources of authority, including newspapers and the experts whose authority they transmit.

The growing popular discontent with the news media has been echoed by a chorus of prominent media critics. Christopher Lasch, James Carey, Jay Rosen, Douglas Kellner, Robert Entman, and others argue that our society faces a crisis of democracy and more broadly a crisis of our social and political institutions. Like many of these critics, Entman, author of *Democracy Without Citizens: Media and the Decay of American Politics*, argues that the news media have played a significant role in creating these crises. They have failed to meet their basic public responsibilities and must redefine their public role if we as a society are to resolve the crises.

Recently, James Fallows's *Breaking the News: How the Media Undermine American Democracy* placed the issue of press responsibilities on the bestseller lists. According to Fallows, "Americans have never been truly fond of their press. Through the last decade, however, their disdain for the media establishment has reached new levels. Americans believe that the news media have become too arrogant, cynical, scandal-minded and destructive."[7] Unless journalism changes, Fallows warns, it will destroy itself and severely damage American democracy.

Critics on the left charge that the American news media have become (or have always been) "stenographers to power," carrying out the agenda of ruling elites. Critics on the right accuse the media of having a liberal social agenda that undermines traditional values. Television journalism in particular has come under attack, accused of distorting public perceptions by dwelling excessively on violent crime.

The growing public hostility toward the press frequently takes the form of demands that journalists live up to the ethical standards of their profession. But the public conception of what those standards are and should be has been largely shaped by the news media themselves.

A closer examination will reveal that the most fundamental problem is not the performance of journalists but the standards themselves. It is quite possible to be a very ethical journalist, relative to the ethical norms that circulate within the profession, and yet to produce journalism that is ineffectual, meaningless, or even irresponsible and destructive, when examined in the light of a broader conception of the ethical responsibilities of the news media.

This irony may explain the widespread cynicism of journalists about the nature of their enterprise and about the role of ethics in journalism. This cynicism is rooted in the profound contradiction between the stated mission of the press, which is to provide citizens with the information they need to play an active role in democratic life, and the reality of daily practice, which systematically compromises values of public service in favor of other interests. Rules theoretically designed to safeguard the stated mission of the press instead frequently serve to legitimate practices that undermine that mission.

The loss of connection and trust between the public and the news media is costly to both citizens and journalists. For citizens, the news media are an important gateway connecting them to their government, their communities, and each other. Journalists need the public even more than the public needs journalism. "It is not only the economy of the newspaper that is at stake when readers turn away," argue Professor Jay Rosen of New York University, a founder of the public journalism movement, and Davis "Buzz" Merritt Jr., senior editor of the *Wichita Eagle*. "It is the foundation of journalism as a public practice. This foundation—a common interest in common affairs—cannot be secured simply by improving the presentation of news, or attending more carefully to what busy readers want. For unless readers also want to be citizens, journalism cannot meet its public responsibilities."[8]

Newspapers will probably survive in some form. The question is whether journalism will survive. When the trends of declining readership, eroding economic base, and the diminishing force of citizenship as a public value are projected out into the future, there is little reason for optimism that the mass-circulation urban newspaper of the future will be any more hospitable to serious journalism than the local television newscast of today.

Are Journalists Listening?

Although much public criticism of the press is now focused on journalism's impact on our democratic institutions and societal values, journalism's institutional conversation about ethics largely ignores these issues. When the three leading figures of journalism's "ethics establishment"—Jay Black, then at the University of Alabama, Bob Steele, of the Poynter Institute for Media Studies, and Ralph Barney, of Brigham Young University— came together in 1993 to create a handbook of journalism ethics, the issues they chose to focus on were largely the same ones that have dominated the institutional conversation for decades: accuracy and fairness, conflicts of interest, deception, plagiarism, and source/reporter relationships.[9] And when the Society of Professional Journalists (SPJ; formerly Society of Professional Journalists/Sigma Delta Chi, or SPJ/SDX) convened in 1996 to revise their code of ethics, they followed the same pattern. Why have these issues, and not those raised by the aforementioned critics, come to dominate the journalism's "official" conversation about ethics?

It might be suggested that this question fuses together two different sets of issues: the matters of daily conduct that concern the ethics establishment and the larger issues of the public responsibilities of the press that concern media critics. But the two sets of issues cannot be so easily separated. The purpose of the rules that govern daily conduct is supposedly to ensure that the press fulfills its public mission. Koppel's remarks suggest that by defining "what's wrong with American journalism today" in terms of individual misconduct, journalism is able to preempt a conversation about the more serious institutional failure.

Journalism's dysfunctional conversation about ethics is at least a contributing cause of its institutional decline. By focusing on the wrong issues, it becomes less able to resist the most serious threats to its vitality and independence or to muster public support.

Taking a Closer Look

The case of Janet Cooke, modern journalism's most famous instance of journalistic misconduct, sheds a great deal of light on how journalism's institutional conversation about ethics operates. Why did this case achieve such singular notoriety? Surely, to choose one example, the failure of the news media to uncover and report the Savings and Loan scandal, described by former *Wall Street Journal* reporter Ellen Hume as "the most expensive public finance debacle in U.S. history,"[10] ranks as a more important ethical issue for journalism than the fictionalizing of a junior *Washington Post* reporter. Why does journalism's internal conversation about ethics focus on Janet Cooke and similar cases while ignoring larger, more systematic shortcomings?

The status of this case cannot really be explained as simply the result of the straightforward application of worthy formal principles. Rather, those principles and rules of conduct are components of a complex system shaped by the institutional interests of the news media and by relations of power within the media. The attention the Cooke case has garnered raises a number of important questions:

- What relationship is there between the principles of ethics expressed in codes of ethics and the rules that govern actual conduct?
- What considerations other than the stated principles help to determine the kinds of cases that get "problematized"—that is, treated as unethical?
- Who decides what the ethical rules are?
- What are the mechanisms by which these values are circulated?
- Who has the authority to determine when an ethical rule has been violated and to decide what sort of sanctions may be imposed?

Answers to these questions help us to understand how journalism ethics, understood as a system of shared values and social practices, operates. But to fully understand the notoriety of the Janet Cooke case, we need to understand not only the rules of journalism's ethical "language game," but also the historical context within which the case arose. What emerges is a picture of journalism ethics as a dysfunctional ethical discourse. That raises a larger question: what kind of conversation about ethics does journalism need, and what conditions must be present for such a conversation to be possible? Answering that question is the focus of this book.

The Organization of the Book

We begin with one basic given: Journalism is in trouble. In the face of declining public respect and interest, journalists are often urged to be more ethical—that is, to adhere more closely to the standards of their profession. But in Chapter 1, where we look more closely at journalism's ethics, it will become apparent that part of the problem may lie with the standards themselves. Journalism's ongoing conversation about ethics turns out to be a very peculiar conversation—inconsistent, sometimes evasive, sometimes strangely silent.

Chapter 2 looks at journalism's ethical conversation at a more formal level, exploring the codes of ethics themselves. These codes also turn out to be problematic—many of the core principles turn out to be ambiguous or even contradictory.

Chapter 3 examines the historical origins of the codes of ethics and the ways in which journalists talk about ethics. Within that context, we visit the Cooke case and find that institutional interests and power relations have always played a strong role in shaping journalism's ethics. The inconsistencies and silences found in journalism's ethical conversation can be seen as distortions produced by institutional interests. At times these inconsistencies may have played a useful role, giving journalists the flexibility to mediate some of the contradictions between theory and practice.

Chapter 4 argues that more recent changes in the newspaper industry are threatening to make journalism's institutional conversation about ethics not merely occasionally inconsistent, but irrelevant, or even meaningless. These changes include the corporate restructuring of newsrooms in ways that reduce the autonomy of journalists and undermine the premise of professionalism on which the codes of ethics are based and the shift by owners to a market-driven philosophy, which undermines the public service ethos.

Journalism's traditional ways of talking about its public responsibilities may be unproductive, or even counter-productive, but there are some deeply held dogmas or myths that stand in the way of change. Chapter 5 looks at one of the core myths—the myth of objectivity, which keeps journalists from finding more productive ways of thinking about and fulfilling their public responsibilities.

Chapter 6 examines and challenges two related doctrines: the dogma of neutrality, which holds that the news media can and should operate outside of the reality that they observe and record, and the information ideology, which treats only the information function of the news media as ethically significant. The argument is made that journalistic objectivity is not possible (that is, that the procedures of journalistic objectivity cannot yield objective truth), that journalists cannot and should not be neutral observers, and that the emphasis on the information function of the news media pays too little attention to the ethical significance of the role that the news media play in shaping public values and individual identity.

Chapter 7 sketches the outlines of a professional ethics for journalism that rests upon a pragmatist theory of knowledge and a more complete account of the role of the news media in society. This approach emphasizes a conception of news as a social construction rather than as an unmediated reflection of reality, based on the assumption that in a society committed to democratic values, the construction of public values should be a democratic process with broad participation. Central to this theory are ethical principles grounded in a different set of values than those behind the prevailing theory.

These new values should include access, diversity, and an emphasis on explanation, context, and narrative as opposed to the conception of news in terms of concrete, discrete events. It is only by adopting these values that the news media can fulfill the role recognized (but inadequately conceptualized) by the traditional social responsibility theory.

Finally, in Chapter 8, we consider the challenges of putting those values into practice. Particular attention is given to the public journalism movement, which acknowledges that journalism has a responsibility for the vitality of public life. At a time when some observers of the press are proclaiming "the end of journalism," this movement may represent the last best hope for the future of journalism as a public practice.

Let us now turn to the initial mystery: How did the case of Janet Cooke become the most famous instance of ethical misconduct in the history of American journalism?

1
How Journalists Talk About Ethics

If there is a word for bad journalism in America, and you look it up in the encyclopedia, and there's Janet Cooke's picture.

—Ted Koppel, ABC *Nightline*, May 10, 1996

Ted Koppel is surely right, but his remark raises an interesting question: With so many Great Moments in Bad Journalism to choose from (not to mention all of the Enduring Disgraces), ranging from the O. J. Simpson media circus to the perennial horse-race coverage of presidential elections and the virtual news blackout on such important (but dull) public issues as the 1996 Telecommunications Act, how did this young black woman manage to capture this distinction? Did she really earn it or could affirmative action be involved? Or might the notoriousness of the Cooke case be an example of what's wrong with the way journalists think about ethics?

The Case of Janet Cooke

In 1981, Janet Cooke, a reporter for the *Washington Post,* was awarded the Pulitzer Prize for a dramatic news story titled "Jimmy's World," purportedly the account of the life of an eight-year-old drug addict. Jimmy was later revealed to be a fictional composite character, the prize was withdrawn, and Cooke resigned in disgrace.

The Janet Cooke scandal has become, quite literally, the textbook example of journalistic misconduct. Virtually every book on media ethics pub-

11

lished since 1981 offers at least a passing reference to the case. The National News Council published a special report on the Cooke case,[1] and the Poynter Institute for Media Studies held a symposium on its impact ten years after the incident. *Media Watch*, a conservative media newsletter, gives a monthly Janet Cooke Award "to distinguish the most outrageously distorted news story of the month."

The Mystery

How did the case of Janet Cooke achieve such notoriety? To answer that question, we need to explore both the history of American journalism and the way that journalism's internal conversation about ethics is conducted. Cooke's status embodies a judgment by American journalism, as an institution, about what is ethically important. Examining her case is a way of exploring how journalism reaches ethical judgments, but it may also offer insight into the factors that shape news judgment generally.

To understand the Cooke case, it is not enough to look at codes of ethics and ethics handbooks, since these documents do not always reflect actual practice. Nor does it suffice to look only at prevailing practices, because some of those practices are contested within the journalism community as unethical. If we turn to what journalists say about the rules that govern their practices, we find that many disagree about the rules and that many of the rules are unspoken.

Thus the ethics of journalism can only be fully explored through the discourse—or conversation—of many, sometimes discordant, voices in codes of ethics and in college textbooks, in editor's memoranda and "underground" newsletters, in ombudsmen's columns, in the minutes of news council meetings, and in reporters' split-second decisions, as well as in coffee-break conversations in newsrooms and in the "Darts and Laurels" column of the *Columbia Journalism Review.*

The Simple Answer

At the Poynter Institute conference, Jay Black, chair of the ethics committee of the Society of Professional Journalists (SPJ) and Poynter-Jamison Chair in Media Ethics at the University of South Florida, offered the conventional explanation of the Cooke affair: "The short, simple answer is that Janet Cooke was a news reporter who did not tell the truth; in so doing, she violated one of the fundamental tenets of journalism."[2]

This interpretation is reflected in the overwhelming majority of writings about the Janet Cooke affair. Stephen Klaidman and Tom Beauchamp, authors of *The Virtuous Journalist*,[3] choose the Cooke case to illustrate their arguments about the importance of trust between reporters and editors. Even though the publication of "Jimmy's World" was the collective responsibility of Cooke and an entire chain of command, the moral significance of the case is interpreted by Klaidman and Beauchamp entirely in terms of Cooke's wrongdoing. "Perhaps it is unfair to *The Washington Post* to recount again Cooke's fictitious reports"[4] they begin, and they go on to analyze the case as an instance of misplaced trust.

Interpretations of the episode vary. In his textbook, *Committed Journalism*, Edmund Lambeth of the University of Missouri uses the Cooke case to discuss the ethics of truth-telling. Cooke's "tragic professional death" comes from her absence of learning, "both cognitive and ethical," of the habit of accuracy. "Deliberate falsification . . . is the most egregious breach of the ethic of truth-telling."[5]

Implicit in the standard explanation is the suggestion that the ostracism of Janet Cooke and the notoriety of her case stem from a straightforward application of well-established rules to a particularly egregious case of misconduct.

Why This Case?

The conventional explanation leaves many important questions unanswered: What is the conception of truth intended in Lambeth's "ethic of truth-telling"? How is this rule applied to particular cases? The conventional explanation, as it stands, cannot adequately account for the singular notoriety of the Cooke case. Does Cooke's behavior really deserve to be counted as the most infamous crime in the history of journalism?

One explanation sometimes offered is that the deception involved the most prestigious prize in American journalism. But this explanation is problematic, given that the fame and importance of the Pulitzer Prize is something that journalism itself has manufactured. Does the status of the Cooke case truly reflect an impartial judgment of its significance or is the indignation greater because journalism's own ox was gored?

Compare the case of Janet Cooke with that of Kurt Lohbeck, a former stringer in Afghanistan for *CBS News*. In a carefully documented report in the *Columbia Journalism Review* (January/February 1990), reporter Mary Ellen Walsh offers evidence that Lohbeck had falsified reports, staged battle scenes, and worked as a publicist for the mujahideen. Lohbeck's fictions continued over a much more extended period than Cooke's, were disseminated to a far larger audience, and were much more substantially false. The basic reality portrayed by Cooke in "Jimmy's World" is true—there are many child victims of the drug epidemic who are in important respects not unlike Cooke's fictional Jimmy. In the case of the Afghan coverage, the coverage was not merely false, it distorted the larger picture, representing the mujahideen as stronger and more unified than they actually were.

In theory, the Lohbeck case ought to rank among the great journalistic scandals of our time. But ultimately, Cooke's case received vastly more media attention. Even within the journalism community the Lohbeck case remains little-known.

One of the few dissenting voices at the Poynter Institute conference on the Cooke affair was Jonathan Kwitny, a former *Wall Street Journal* reporter and host of a public television news program. "The Cooke episode raised no question worth debating, save maybe the values of checking the pedigree of new hires a bit more carefully," argued Kwitny in a speech titled "The Ethics of Ownership." "In the most fundamentally ethical society we could create, every now and again some human misfit would still rob a bank, murder a spouse, or even, yes, lie to a newspaper."[6]

Kwitny argues that there are cases that present much more serious violations of the public's right to know and of the news media's duty to inform the public. "Why did the biggest stories in recent years—the Iran Contra scandal, Gorbachev's moves to end the Cold War, the savings-and-loan catastrophe and the collapse of communism in Eastern Europe . . . come as total shocks to the public, even though evidence of all of these events had long been developing?"[7]

The result of this failure to report, argues Kwitny, "was that American interests may have been damaged for years by the continuation of outmoded policies." These are, Kwitny suggests, more significant consequences than any that may have resulted from Janet Cooke's story. By failing to adequately inform the American public about these events, the news media deprived the public of its right to play its proper role in self-governance.

Kwitny's explanation for these failures of journalistic responsibility have to do with who owns the media and the subservience of journalism to economic interests. And that raises a different set of issues that he believes should be put on the ethical agenda for journalists: the social responsibilities of news media owners.

But the fact remains that the Cooke case has achieved legendary status, while the Lohbeck case and the cases Kwitny cites are either ignored or regarded as ethically insignificant. Why is it that fictional reporting is considered a violation of the "ethic of truth-telling," but the failure to investigate the truthfulness of one's sources is not? Why are the economic prerogatives of owners generally excluded from the institutionalized discourse of journalism ethics? In order to explain, we need to look at the kinds of cases that journalists do talk about and to explore how the more abstract foundational principles of professional ethics are translated into procedural rules. It is important to have not only an understanding of how the formal rules are interpreted, but also an understanding of power relationships in journalism and the historical context in which the concepts and forces shaping the institutionalized ethical discourse developed.

What emerges from such inquiry is a picture of journalism ethics, like perhaps all professional ethics, as a *self-interested* discourse, motivated by the institutional priorities of the participants and subject to conflicts, incoherencies, and silences at junctures where those interests conflict. This is a very different sort of discourse than the disinterested inquiry into the nature of the good that is held to be an ideal of ethical reasoning. (We may set aside the question of whether that ideal is ever realized in practice.)

To put it in other terms, since all discourse is in some sense interested, that is, motivated by human interests, this is not a discourse motivated by a quest to seek the common interest, but rather one that uses the vocabulary of moral discourse to advance particular interests. The ethics of journalism are not very different than the ethics of law or medicine in this regard, but journalism is unique in its capacity to shape public values and to mold public opinion about the standards to which it should be held.

Ethics in Theory and Practice

The kind of ethical discourse or conversation that takes place on a daily basis among working journalists is different from the more abstract and theoretical discourse that can be found in codes of ethics, in papers given at professional conferences, and in other official venues. Although we can refer to this distinction in terms of the practical and the theoretical, the practical discourse is not simply an elaboration of the principles expressed in the codes of ethics, nor are the codes and similar statements merely attempts to capture in theoretical terms a set of values widely held by practitioners.

The ways journalists report and edit are shaped by the relations of power and by the institutional priorities within the organizations that employ them. These relations and priorities are not in equilibrium, but exist in an ongoing state of conflict. Thus, the institutional values of journalism are not grounded in a static set of rules but rather emerge from an evolving set of practices. These values are transmitted by individual working journalists whose actions are constrained and defined by the dynamics of concrete real-life situations. In so far as ethical rules can be identified, they must be understood as emerging from these practices and contexts, subject to interpretation in concrete situations.

An action or practice becomes an ethical issue when it is made problematic in an ethical discourse. Such a discourse is structured—there are rules about what may be said and who is privileged to speak. Only the executive editor is privileged to speak in an editor's memorandum, and what he or she may say is constrained by the relationships that exist between publisher, editor, newsroom staff, and the public. In order for an issue to achieve the status of being ethically problematic, there must exist an appropriate forum for the generation of such a discussion.

The SPJ Code of Ethics is produced by the ethics committee of the organization, whose primary mission is to promote recognition of journalism as a profession. This mission is reflected in the selection of issues that it chooses to acknowledge as ethical and the issues that it does not address.

The ethical criticisms expressed in "The Downward Spiral," published sporadically by a small group of disaffected employees of the *Detroit Free Press* in the mid-80s, reflected a somewhat different set of priorities—a defense of traditional "hard news" values against a marketing-oriented corporate ownership. Nearly all of the articles that appeared in "The Downward Spiral" were unsigned; the need for anonymity imposed a complex set of restrictions on what might be said and limited participation to those journalists willing to accept the attendant risks.

Theory As It Relates to Practice

It is not enough to describe the various things that journalists say in different contexts of institutional power about professional ethics. We also need to develop a theory of how these utterances are related and interpreted. If we speak of this larger discourse as an apparatus, our task is to understand how the apparatus works. Some components may prove to be more important than others, and some things that journalists say about ethics may prove to be purely ceremonial or even insincere.

Thus, a useful treatment of the ethics of journalism must encompass all of its components, including the contexts from which those ethics emerge. Within the more theoretical component of prescriptive principles and rules, there are several levels of abstraction or generality—a theory of the social responsibility of the media, a stratum of principles, and a set of procedural rules that operationalize those principles. Two key issues are the relationship between theory and practice and the relationships between the theoretical propositions at various levels, for example, how a principle of fairness comes to be equated with rules of procedure a, b, and c, and not rules d, e, and f. Ultimately, all the components must be drawn together to create an overall picture of the origins and workings of journalism ethics.

Practice: The Ethical Discourse

When journalists talk about ethics, they mostly talk about cases—either cases of misconduct or cases that represent a conflict between two competing journalistic rules or values. Like everybody else, they tend to talk about the cases that are in the news—media coverage of the private lives of politicians, whether reporters should have the right to make promises of confidentiality, or whether the page-one photograph of the grieving family was an excessive intrusion into private grief.

It is possible to distinguish between cases that have what might be termed "official" recognition as ethically significant—the kinds of cases that get discussed at ethics conferences, in ethics reports, and in professional journals—and another class of cases that are marginalized—the kinds of cases that journalists discuss sotto voce, cases whose very status as ethical is contested.

Officially Recognized Cases

The internal discourse over journalistic dilemmas and misconduct takes place at ethics workshops, in the pages of journals, in disciplinary actions taken in newsrooms, in the meetings of news councils, and in reports by the various professional organizations, such as the American Society of Newspaper Editors (ASNE) and the SPJ.

Since the late 1970s, concern within the journalism community over ethics has increased greatly, as the Watergate affair increased public and journalistic awareness of the ethical conflicts that arise from the complex relationship of the news media to the nation's political institutions. But the ethical categories established by the codes—conflict of interest, invasion of privacy, sensationalism, truthfulness and accuracy—with few exceptions still set the agenda for criticism of journalistic conduct, at least in determining in a general way the kinds of cases that are worthy of attention, if not in selecting which particular cases will be treated as ethically problematic.

The Cooke case clearly falls within the framework established by the codes, but so do all of the other cases that have received widespread attention. The right of reporters to maintain confidentiality of news sources was the central issue in another ethics case that received national publicity—Dan Cohen's lawsuit against the *Minneapolis Star and Tribune* (now the *Star Tribune*) and *St. Paul Pioneer Press-Dispatch* (now the *St. Paul Pioneer Press*). In this case, editors reneged on promises made by reporters not to reveal the identity of a Republican political operative who furnished the newspapers with damaging information about the criminal record of a Democratic politician.

The most widely publicized case of conflict of interest in recent years is perhaps that of R. Foster Winans, reporter for the *Wall Street Journal,* who eventually served time in prison for giving insider information to a stockbroker.

The issue of sensationalism was in the media spotlight during and after the 1988 presidential campaign, when the private life of Senator Gary Hart came under extensive media scrutiny, and again during the 1992 campaign, when Bill Clinton came under similar scrutiny. The attention given to their alleged extramarital relationships sometimes overshadowed coverage of many of the more substantive issues of the campaign. Ethical concern focused on the right to privacy of a public figure (in the case of Hart), the reliability of the news sources (in the case of Clinton), and whether the coverage of the candidates' personal lives was disproportionate to its political importance. Several recent lawsuits, including Food Lion's successful suit against ABC, have brought the issue of deception to the forefront.

Whatever the professional norms may be or have been, those cases and others suggest that when the news is "hot" enough, there is always a way to justify publication without violating the rules of the game. The private peccadilloes of Hart and Clinton were justified as newsworthy because of the light they might shed on the candidates' characters. And although an allegation of impropriety in a tabloid weekly might not meet the standards of evidence traditionally required by the mainstream press, editors who wish to report allegations can circumvent the standards by treating the publishing of the allegations as itself newsworthy.

Throughout the 1980s, the SPJ published annual ethics reports. The *1989 Ethics Report* is typical—a collection of essays and reprinted newspaper articles on a wide range of topics from "Covering the AIDS Crisis" to "The Impact of Advertising." Virtually all of the cases discussed fall into the categories noted above. The use of unattributed and off-the-record information (fairness and accuracy) is discussed in three separate essays. A report about a television reporter who posed for *Playboy,* accompanied by a large photograph of the magazine cover, discusses whether such activity diminishes the credibility of female reporters (sensationalism). Two articles explore when it is permissible or appropriate to present as a direct quote material that is either paraphrased or grammatically improved (accuracy).

Other issues explored include the use of new technology to alter photographs (accuracy), the issue of privacy in reporting AIDS deaths, and the particular ethical problems that confront sports writers (conflict of interest). Issues of economics are dealt with in two articles: one on "how financial and circulation imperatives can distort reporting of a story" and one on the increasingly blurred line between editorial and advertising departments (conflict of interest).

Although public and internal discourse about journalism ethics tends to focus on cases of misconduct, much attention is also given to ethical dilemmas—what happens when two or more of these fundamental principles come into conflict. In college textbooks and in ethics workshops sponsored by newspapers and journalism institutes, ethical dilemmas in journalism are often discussed using real or fictional case studies.

Fine Line, a short-lived publication that described itself as "The Newsletter on Journalism Ethics," was largely devoted to discussion of real-life situations faced by journalists. Among the dilemmas discussed in a typical issue (January 1990):

- Should a television report on a crisis in psychiatric care report a suicide by name, against the widow's wishes? (The widow's right to privacy versus the public's right to know.)
- Should a reporter assist in apprehending a fleeing suspect? (The duties of citizenship versus the requirements of objectivity.) If he does, may he then report the arrest on television? (Issues of objectivity and conflict of interest.)
- Should a newspaper withhold information that could precipitate a run on a local bank? (The public's right to know versus the duty to avoid harm.)

If these are the kinds of cases that journalists talk about, what do they say about them? In a surprising number of cases, they actually say very little.

Conversations About Ethics

The Case of the Playmate Reporter

Lauren Millette, author of the SPJ/SDX report on the Playmate news reporter Shelly Jamison, declines to draw any ethical conclusions about the incident, opting instead to report the incident in straightforward news style. She quotes the television station's general manager, Ron Bergamo, who shows a similar reluctance: "From an ethical standpoint, it's somewhat interesting. What we would have done for disciplinary action is a tough question. Because most of her job responsibilities were as a producer, we probably wouldn't have had a problem with it ethically. But she misrepresented herself."[8]

Bergamo's concern is that by representing herself as a full-time reporter, Jamison may have damaged the station's credibility: "All newscasters young and old have a responsibility to be as credible as possible in their personal life as well as their professional life," he comments. Jamison's view is more cynical, according to Millette: "Jamison said sex is a product just like television anchors are a product. If someone is going to capitalize off her talents, it might as well be her."[9]

The Case of Donna Rice

The same reluctance to draw ethical conclusions is evident in a report on an unannounced appearance at a journalism ethics convention by Donna Rice, who gained a brief moment of public notoriety because of her relationship with presidential candidate Gary Hart. The story, by Jim Mann, assistant managing editor of the Fredricksburg, Virginia, *Free-Lance Star*, reports that Rice twice requested that her remarks be kept "off the record," and that several reporters nonetheless filed stories quoting her.[10] Mann quotes a letter to the editor written by a minister who attended the session that sharply criticized *Richmond Times-Dispatch* reporter Rob Walker for not honoring Rice's request, but the journalists quoted in the story are less forthcoming. A *Times-Dispatch* editor comments that Rice "preferred that her remarks not be reported, but there was no prohibition." Reporter

Bruce Potter of the rival *Richmond News Leader* also evades the issue, insisting repeatedly that the failure to announce before the start of the session (rather than at the start) that Rice's comments were off the record made for a "very confusing situation."

Drawing a Fine Line

The *Fine Line* discussions of dilemmas are often equally unsatisfying. Some of them sound like ex post facto rationalizations, while others simply seem evasive; few really attempt to engage the central problems in a sustained and constructive way. In the case of the suicide, the suicide's sister was interviewed on camera, contrary to the widow's wishes, but the family was not identified. Here is the reporter's assessment: "My advice? There are no fixed ethical rules for TV journalists. The balance between public good and private pain is a delicate one. You have to find it each time you turn your camera on a tragedy that needs to be exposed."[11]

In the case of the fleeing suspect, the television reporter stopped the suspect while his cameraman filmed the action, and his station then showed the unedited tape on the nightly news. The reporter's comment:

> My own feeling is that my reaction was the right one for me. In my mind, there is little difference between jumping in front of a fleeing suspect and a story that points the finger at those guilty of environmental pollution, or graft, or murder.
>
> In any case, the action serves the public interest. And that is what this business is supposed to be about: serving the public.
>
> In this case, it was just a little more dramatic and a little more direct.[12]

The Poynter Institute has emerged as the leading center for journalism ethics in the United States, and the director of their ethics programs, Bob Steele, has become one of the most widely cited experts on journalism ethics. Newspapers and television stations from all over the United States send reporters and editors to attend their week-long workshops on ethical decision-making, and the center recently established a Web site devoted to journalism ethics.

A visit to the Poynter Web site gives a sampling of the kinds of cases that are treated as ethically significant: The case of Cheryl Ann Barnes, a Florida teenager whose disappearance prompted a media "feeding frenzy"; the case of security guard Richard Jewell, falsely suspected of planting a bomb during the Olympic Games in Atlanta; and a discussion of how the

New York Times and *Washington Post* should have responded to the Unabomber's demand that they publish his manifesto.

The Poynter study of the Cheryl Ann Barnes case, written by Poynter Institute Associate Scott Libin and Jay Black, offers considerable detail on the facts of the case.[13] The case was initially covered as an abduction and generated intense local and regional coverage. When Barnes was discovered in New York City, suffering from amnesia, the local media pooled resources to charter a plane and fly Barnes's family and their reporters to cover the hospital reunion. Libin and Black quote a February 11 report in the *St. Petersburg Times* by Andrew Galarneau as saying that "When Cheryl came home, she was greeted by five TV satellite trucks with crews, 11 roving camera teams, and photographers and reporters for at least seven newspapers, including the New York Daily News." Later evidence emerged that indicated that Barnes had a very troubled home life and was more likely a runaway than an abductee.

The Poynter discussion of the (ethical) issues in the case begins with dozens of questions:

> Did the media ask enough questions? Should reporters have pressed for further insight from police and deputies as to why they believed someone had abducted Cheryl? . . . Were they too accepting of the official account because it made for a more compelling story?
>
> What if police had said there was a good chance Cheryl was a runaway? Most news organizations don't routinely cover such cases. (The most common reasons are that there are too many runaways, and that coverage sometimes encourages other kids. . . .)[14]

The case study does not attempt to answer these questions. This is consistent with a larger pattern in the way journalists and journalism scholars talk about ethics: They frequently show a great reluctance to make ethical judgments. It could be argued that the purpose of a case study is simply to raise questions, but in that case, it is fair to ask whether the right questions are being raised.

Implicit in the pattern of questions is the assumption that if the case had indeed been a kidnapping, the amount of attention given to it by the media would have been appropriate—although some of the particular conduct of the media might still be questionable. What is not discussed, even as a question, is how the coverage of this event serves the public interest, as opposed to satisfying the public's curiosity. What legitimate public interest is served by covering this story so extensively? We are not told—nor even asked—how the amount of attention and resources devoted to the coverage of this story might compare with the coverage the television stations and newspapers involved have given to critical public issues in areas such as government or public safety.

Although Libin and Black leave their questions unanswered, they do point the reader in the direction of solutions:

> Drawing from work developed by the Poynter Institute and Society of Professional Journalists (see Jay Black, Bob Steele, and Ralph Barney, *Doing Ethics in Journalism: A Manual with Case Studies*, 2d ed. [Needham Heights, MA: 1995]), a thoughtful set of resolutions to the above issues could be managed by balancing some conflicting principles and answering a set of questions.

Seek a Balance Among Sometimes Conflicting Principles

First, journalists should recognize that doing an ethical job entails seeking a balance among three guiding principles:

1. seeking and reporting as much truthful, accurate, and significant news as possible by using honest, fair, and courageous newsgathering and reporting methods;
2. acting independently from sources, subjects, and others who would unfairly manipulate the news coverage to their own advantages and counter to the public interest;
3. minimizing the harm and discomfort that journalism often entails, and treat sources, subjects, and colleagues as human beings deserving of respect, not merely as means to journalistic ends.

These three principles are often in conflict with one another. Such was surely the case for the six weeks during which the Cheryl Ann Barnes story was being played out.

Ask Good Questions to Make Good Ethical Decisions

1. What do I know? What do I need to know?
2. What is my journalistic purpose?
3. What are my ethical concerns?
4. What organizational policies and professional guidelines should I consider?
5. How can I include other people, with different perspectives and diverse ideas, in the decision-making process?
6. Who are the stakeholders—those affected by my decision? What are their motivations? Which are legitimate?

7. What if the roles were reversed? How would I feel if I were in the shoes of one of the stakeholders?
8. What are the possible consequences of my actions? Short term? Long term?
9. What are my alternatives to maximize my truth-telling responsibility and minimize harm?
10. Can I clearly and fully justify my thinking and my decision? To my colleagues? To the stakeholders? To the public?[15]

These are all good questions, but Libin and Black do not try to show how they will generate solutions, and their own solution suggests that the products of such reflection may not really be the important issue in any case:

> The audience will rule on the media's performance. Viewers, as Channel 28 News Director Bob Jordan says, "vote with the remote [control]," and, in the free market of commercial television, those votes count more than all the academic analysis in the world. Subsequent, separate controversies have arisen among the same TV news operations from stories unrelated to the Barnes saga even since we started work on this case study, giving viewers even more opportunities to judge those who compete for their business. Ultimately, the signals the audience sends back to the broadcasters will determine the direction in which this market's mass media head from here.[16]

But if that is the case, then ethical reflection is irrelevant. Surely, if there is any point in ethical reflection, ethics seminars, and the whole discourse of journalism ethics, it must be to identify those points where journalists must follow principle rather than the dictates of the marketplace.

Moreover, Black and Libin seem to be suggesting that in choosing to watch one station over another, viewers are making an implied judgment about the journalistic quality of the stations' reporting. This seems to ignore the possibility that the public may be making its choices on the basis of some criterion other than journalistic excellence or that the judgment of the public, which relies on trust in journalists, might be mistaken.

Bob Steele's discussion of the Unabomber case offers a more detailed look at how the ten "good questions" and the principles of truth-seeking, minimizing harm, and independence are supposed to generate answers to ethical dilemmas. "The guiding principles of truth-seeking and truth-telling along with journalistic independence provide a moral compass that decision-makers can turn to for guidance," Steele writes.

> This moral compass does not dictate specific action. It does provide essential reference points. . . . The benefit of doing ethical decision-making as a

process is that it almost always creates a range of potential courses of action. We should then hold these various choices up against our guiding principles. The decision-maker's goal is to choose an alternative that best honors those guiding principles, recognizing that these principles are sometimes in competition with each other.[17]

But when Steele generates a list of possible actions that the newspapers could take, they seem more like ways of avoiding acting on principle:

Among the alternatives in this case:

- Buy time by making no final decision right now. The Unabomber gave the *Times* and the *Post* three months to publish his manifesto. By taking time before they make a final decision the newspapers may open up other possibilities, including the chance that the Unabomber is apprehended.
- Try to open a conversation with the Unabomber to see if there are other courses of action that might be possible short of giving in to his demands. Negotiation is often the pathway to resolution.
- Take some small steps related to his demands, possibly publishing some excerpts from his manifesto. Such actions may be justifiable journalistically based on the newsworthiness of those excerpts, thereby eliminating some of the negative consequences that come with giving in to terrorist demands.
- Continue behind-the-scenes consultation with law enforcement and governmental authorities in order to reduce the chance that the papers will do something that interferes with the investigation or something that further infuriates the Unabomber, leading to more harm to the public.
- Go ahead and publish the complete manifesto, but in a form other than the daily newspaper. That publishing might be in book form, or on the Internet, or in mass distribution of copies of the manifesto.
- Go ahead and publish the complete manifesto in the newspaper, but make it very clear to the public that this was an absolutely last choice given the nature of this case and that the decision to publish will carry no weight in terms of precedence.[18]

The first solution, buying time, amounts to stalling and hoping the problem goes away—perhaps not a bad solution, but it is not clear that the apparatus of ethical decision making is necessary or helpful in reaching it. The second solution, negotiating with the Unabomber, begs the question: Which principles should the newspaper be prepared to compromise and to what extent? "Taking small steps" poses similar problems. The claim that the excerpts are being published, at this particular moment, solely on the basis of their newsworthiness, is not likely to be convincing to the journalists involved or to anyone else.

Publishing the manifesto, but in some other form, seems a case of trying to have one's ethical cake and eat it too: to satisfy the Unabomber's demands and yet be able to deny that one has. And publishing the full text in the newspaper and then telling the public that no precedent has been set seems to be merely a case of wishful thinking—of course, a precedent will have been set.

Going Beyond Cases

If journalists and journalism educators have a difficult time talking in a productive way about cases, they have an even more difficult time going beyond cases and discussing professional ethics on a more abstract level. Those who do seem to have an odd fondness for metaphor. The anonymous author of the preface to an undated SPJ/SDX ethics report laments that "coming to grips with journalism ethics is like shaking hands with a jellyfish." John Merrill calls journalism ethics "a swampland of philosophical speculation where eerie mists of judgment hang low over a boggy terrain."[19]

Those who do venture into this challenging terrain sometimes get hopelessly lost. Consider, for example, the advice offered to journalists by Ben Johnson, associate professor of journalism at the University of Missouri, in an article published in a 1989 SPJ/SDX report:

Ethics are nothing more than being fair. Follow these suggestions.

- Establish a set of rules. They should be more guidelines, than commandments. . . .
- Be prepared to handle each situation on a case by case basis. Few ethical rules should be drafted that make clearly right and wrong determinations. Most cases are invariably somewhere in the middle.
- For example, plagiarism is wrong. Most good journalists would agree. One should never "borrow" the work of another without attribution. But would an editor handle a brand-new reporter guilty of plagiarizing the same way one would handle a veteran?

    The clear answer should be no. A staff member just learning a job should be accorded more latitude than one who already knows the job. What about the staffer writing obituaries? Isn't a clip job plagiarism? Does changing one word per paragraph make it okay?

- Rule by example. A newspaper which has a fairly strict prohibition on accepting anything of value from news sources sends the wrong message if top editors feel free to accept such gratuities. Likewise, this same newspaper should not allow those on the advertising staff to accept gifts from clients.

The bottom line is to make sure that you're [sic] ethics can't be questioned.[20]

The careful reader may be puzzled by some of Johnson's formulations. How is it possible that "most cases are invariably in the middle?" When he writes "clearly right and wrong determinations," does he mean "clear determinations of right and wrong?" Does he really believe that a clear and concise prohibition of plagiarism would require all infractions to be handled in the same way? Does he confuse a "clip job" (writing a story entirely from secondary sources) with plagiarism (failure to give appropriate attribution)? Can a newspaper where top editors feel free to accept gratuities really be said to have a strict policy on that issue?

It is important not to misconstrue the function or importance of reports like the one just cited. Although the material is presented in the form of a manual of moral instruction, it is unlikely that anyone reads it for such purposes. It is unlikely, in fact, that very many people read such a piece at all. The relative impact of the report or of the SPJ on the practice of journalism is negligible, yet the report is revealing.

Why Journalists Can't Theorize

Explanations of Journalistic Incoherence

There are a number of theories, all worthy of consideration, about why journalists have so much difficulty articulating coherent visions of their social responsibilities. One theory, derived from the work of philosopher Alasdair MacIntyre, is that the incoherence of journalistic discourse about professional ethics is merely a reflection of a larger societal incoherence with respect to moral discourse. MacIntyre suggests that this incoherence is the product of a philosophical confusion that results from the encounter in public discourse of several competing and incompatible philosophical traditions.[21] An alternative possibility is that the incoherence of moral discourse in both the media and the larger society may be partly attributable to the mass media themselves, which have an intrinsic tendency to break down walls between communities with different moral norms.

There may also be specific institutional factors that explain the silences and incoherencies in journalism's ethical discourse. The set of practices that constitute journalistic objectivity have built into them a bias against explicit moral judgments. Journalists are conditioned to see such judgments as subjective and to edit them out of their stories, unless they can attribute them to a source. One result of this is that a number of the most famous cases of ethics are grounded in judgments generated elsewhere, for example, the Dan Cohen and Foster Winans cases, where legal rulings offer a basis or at least a substitute for moral judgment.

Another set of explanations is offered by James Carey of Columbia University. His essay, "Journalists Just Leave,"[22] takes its title from a remark made by Arthur Caplan, former associate director of the Hastings Center. Caplan once observed that although nearly all other professional groups that attend conferences at the center go on to start ethics study groups, organizations, or journals, or engage in other forms of ethical discourse, journalists simply leave and are never heard from again. Carey's explanations are that (1) neither journalists nor philosophers know how to talk about journalism ethics; (2) journalists fear that to entertain public discussion of their professional ethics is the first step down the road to increased regulation; (3) because journalism is a far more public activity than, for example, medicine, journalists feel more exposed and more defensive about their practices; and (4) unlike the doctors, lawyers, and ministers who provide the model for discussion of professional ethics, journalists are not independent practitioners serving individual clients, but rather hired hands working for large organizations and serving an amorphous public.

The theory that journalists do not know how to talk about professional ethics may well be true, but it does not provide a complete explanation for the character of the institutionalized discourse. We must also consider the possibility that journalists use the language of morality for purposes other than a disinterested inquiry into the nature of the right and the good, and that these other uses may distort or compete with efforts to develop theories of professional responsibility. In an essay entitled "Objectivity as Strategic Ritual,"[23] sociologist Gaye Tuchman has argued that journalists use the practices of objectivity as a shield to fend off criticism. Similarly, James Carey argues that "the ethics of journalism often seem to be a cover, a means of avoiding the deeper questions in order to concentrate on a few problems on which there is general agreement, though of course the flesh, as usual, is weak."[24]

There may also be another explanation or at least another way of describing the explanation to which Carey seems to be pointing: Journalists have a difficult time talking coherently about professional ethics because there are fundamental incoherencies or contradictions built into the core principles of the profession. In order to explore this thesis, we need to examine how these principles are formulated and how they are interpreted in practice.

Marginalized Cases

The cases discussed above, which are acknowledged within the profession as ethically significant and discussed as such in officially sanctioned forums, can be contrasted with a second class of cases, which are marginalized. These kinds of cases, for a variety of reasons, usually do not get circulated in the same ways as the kinds of cases described above, and their very status as ethical issues is sometimes contested. These cases tend to involve categories that are generally recognized as significant within the news media, such as conflict of interest or editorial independence from advertisers, or issues such as racism, sexism, or ideological bias that have not traditionally been recognized as ethical categories in journalism. Let us explore how these categories and issues enter into the everyday decisions of journalists.

Conflict of Interest.   The following are some typical instances in which an apparent conflict of interest might arise:

- A newspaper publisher accepts an assignment from the embattled governor of the state to act as press coordinator for a visit by a foreign dignitary. Reporters worry that such an arrangement creates a conflict of interest and has a potentially chilling impact on news coverage. For example, the publisher may then have a vested interest in seeing that the visit is perceived as a success.
- An executive editor is named vice president in charge of circulation, breaching the traditional separation between editorial and business operations. Reporters worry that the editor's news judgment will be compromised by his responsibility to promote circulation growth.
- A newspaper signs a contract for exclusive rights to promote a local basketball team on company-owned billboards, in newspaper ads,

and in other media. Sports columnists complain that the contract undermines their credibility as journalists.

- An editor deletes information about a fur protest from an article about fur fashions that appears on the cover of a feature section. The offending material appears a day later in a less prominent location. The editor explains that advertisers bought space in the section with a reasonable expectation that their ads would not appear in a hostile editorial environment.

Editorial Independence from Advertisers.   Advertisers are not explicitly mentioned in any of the major codes of ethics, but relationships between editorial content and advertisers are a major ethical concern among journalists and a frequent topic of the *Columbia Journalism Review* "Darts and Laurels" column. The kind of case that is recognized as unethical typically involves a publisher or editor directly intervening in the editorial process to secure favorable treatment for an advertiser. Those kinds of cases are recognized as ethically significant within the profession, but other cases that raise questions of editorial independence are not. The following examples serve to illustrate:

- Newspaper travel sections typically publish several cruise sections every year. The number of cruise sections is not determined by reader interest, but rather by the advertising department, based on the availability of advertising dollars. There is an understanding between the advertising department and advertisers that negative stories about cruises, cruise safety, and such will not appear in the special cruise sections.
- Newspaper automotive sections typically feature reviews (almost invariably favorable) of a new car borrowed for reviewing purposes from a local dealer.
- At one large newspaper, the executive editor accompanies the newspaper's largest advertiser, who is owner of a supermarket chain and an active supporter of Israeli causes, on a trip to Israel. Upon his return he writes a series of front page stories about the conflicts in the region.
- The *New York Times, Los Angeles Times,* and other newspapers regularly produce "branded products," special sections produced by the newsroom staff that as a matter of policy do not carry any negative, critical, or watchdog stories. Although these sections are usually la-

beled in some way to indicate that they are not traditional news sections, it is not clear exactly what the distinction is that is being made or how well the distinction is understood by readers. Calling these sections "branded products" attaches the credibility of the newspaper's brand name to the product. Further complicating the picture is the fact that many newspapers also publish "advertorial" sections, produced by the advertising department, with text designed to support the advertising content. Although these sections are usually labeled as advertising supplements, that distinction may also be lost on readers, especially since they are presented in a journalistic format.

Journalists are well aware of the ethical problems that advertorial sections and "branded products" represent. At one major Midwestern daily newspaper, the leadership of the Newspaper Guild issued a statement of concern:

> We feel that these special sections do undermine the journalistic integrity of the newspaper, and we fear that they will divert more and more advertising from the news pages. We ask: Will we wind up with a few news pages surrounded by only "happy news?" Will the special sections produced in the newsroom, Homes and Home and Garden, be squeezed out by the competition from our own advertising department? Will advertisers come to expect that "good" stories will run alongside their ads?[25]

Allocation of Resources. Another part of the puzzle is how the news media opt to utilize the space or other resources available to them. The following examples illustrate the potential problems that may arise:

- Every day for a week the news hole in the A section (national, international, and major local news stories) is smaller than the news hole for sports. The strategy gives preferential treatment to a class of readers perceived as demographically desirable.
- A newspaper publisher announces a $1 million cut in newsroom budget. This necessitates the elimination of approximately fifteen journalists from the staff and the elimination of the zoned section, which is the principal space in the newspaper for community news. The publisher insists that the cuts are necessary because of declining revenues—the newspaper's annual return is in danger of falling below 10 percent, a level that is unacceptable to the company's stockholders.

Failure to Cover. "Errors of omission far outnumber mistakes of commission in 1990s journalism," says one veteran reporter.

> What we don't write would fill a book. To a degree, that's always been true. But more so now. When's the last time you read a consumer story about the misdeeds of a local car dealer? Or an examination of what lobbyists for insurance companies, utilities and other companies regulated by state government did to consumers in the last session of the legislature?[26]

A survey of coverage of the 1994 Congressional races found that the *New York Times* failed to publish a single full-length article about 11 of the 20 Congressional races in its local circulation area (some races were covered in round-up pieces), while the *Los Angeles Times* similarly neglected some 11 of the 23 races in its local circulation area.

Issues of Sexism and Racism. The 1996 revision of the SPJ Code of Ethics was the first to explicitly address the issue of racism, counseling journalists to "avoid stereotyping by race, gender, age, religion, ethnicity, geography, sexual orientation, disability, physical appearance or social status." Racism and sexism are sometimes acknowledged as ethical issues because a law-suit has drawn attention to a case (for example, the firing of television news anchor Christine Craft, who was dismissed for being "too old, too ugly, and not deferential to men"). But even when these issues are acknowledged as ethically significant, they are given a very narrow definition. Thus, explicitly racist remarks or discriminatory hiring practices are recognized and criticized, but definitions of news that give communities of color media attention only in the context of stories about drugs, crime, or welfare are not regarded as ethically problematic. There are a variety of cases that do not receive such recognition:

- A newspaper devotes an extended series of articles to following a single African-American teenager through her pregnancy and the birth of her child. Although the treatment is sympathetic, the local African-American community is outraged. In the context of the virtual invisibility of African-Americans in the paper, the series only confirms stereotypes and reinforces prejudices.
- According to the study "Gender Stereotyping in Televised Sports," published by the Amateur Athletic Foundation of Los Angeles, broadcasters covering the 1989 U.S. Open Finals typically referred to male athletes by their last names and to female athletes by their first names.

"When men were referred to by first name only, the players were always men of color."[27]

These marginalized cases differ from the more widely publicized cases in that, although from the standpoint of an outside observer they may seem to at least raise serious ethical issues or in some instances to involve clear cases of misconduct, within the institution their very status as ethical issues is not acknowledged. But to better understand what counts as an ethical issue and what does not, we need to take a closer look at journalism's codes of ethics.

2

Talking in Code(s): The Foundations of Journalism Ethics

Although the daily discourse of journalism ethics that takes place in newsrooms and in the pages of professional journals is full of contradictions and silences, there is an underlying set of values that shapes journalists' understanding of where the boundaries are drawn. This core set of values is given expression in journalism's codes of ethics. Hardly anyone ever reads codes of journalism ethics, but it would be a mistake to underestimate their importance. Not many people read the U.S. Constitution or the Magna Carta either, and yet those documents continue to exercise a profound impact on our culture.

The fundamental principles expressed in journalism's codes of ethics are supposed to provide the basis for ethical decision-making. Instead, they embody some of the ambiguities and contradictions that lie at the heart of journalism. In times of relative stability, those ambiguities and inconsistencies may in fact have been more a solution than a problem—they provided a tool with which journalists could mediate some of the contradictions between theory and practice. But in times of rapid change, in which journalism is facing both structural changes that threaten its integrity as a social practice and a public that is increasingly dissatisfied with journalism's performance, this traditional institutional ethical discourse becomes not simply irrelevant, but an actual impediment to journalists being able to respond to those structural challenges and external critics.

In the fall of 1996, the ethics committee of the SPJ revised the society's Code of Ethics for the first time since 1987. The nine intervening years were among the most turbulent in journalism's history. Consolidation of newspaper ownership continued, and in many cases new owners slashed newsroom staffs and reduced news holes in the quest for higher profits. Many newsrooms were restructured, with new systems of organization that reduced the autonomy of the individual reporter. (For an organization whose very name has embodied the contentious claim that journalists are professionals, this erosion of autonomy should be of particular concern.) Market research increasingly replaced traditional judgments of newsworthiness in editorial decision-making. The focus at many newspapers shifted from informing the citizen to serving the customer.

None of these changes, which go to the heart of the practice of journalism, are addressed by the new, revised code. "The SPJ Code is aimed at individual journalists; it's not written for organizations or institutions," explains SPJ President Steve Geimann. "We've tried to cover the bases as they pertain to working professional journalists today. . . . A code of ethics shouldn't be a checklist of do's and don'ts. Instead, it should be a set of guidelines that can help responsible journalists be more responsible, be more accountable to their profession and to their audience. I think the Code does that."[1]

Although the new SPJ Code admonishes journalists to "act independently," and to "deny favored treatment to advertisers and special interests," no mention is made of the threats to independence posed by the increasing influence of the newspaper's own advertising and marketing departments or the loss of independence that can occur when a newspaper becomes a subsidiary of a chain or media conglomerate.

During the period between revisions of the SPJ Code of Ethics, critics of the press became more vocal and numerous: James Fallows wrote a best-selling book, *Breaking the News: How the Media Undermine American Democracy*, in which he charged that the media have become arrogant, cynical, scandal-minded, and destructive. Journalism, he charged, has embraced a star system that has created a class of celebrity journalists whose own wealth distorts their perceptions of the needs and concerns of their audience. "The status revolution in big-time journalism has given many reporters a strong if unconscious bias in favor of 'haves' rather than 'have nots.'"[2]

Fallows described the ways in which the financial rewards for achieving star status distort journalistic practice: The journalist with a clever quip or sharp put-down can become a celebrity on the talk-show circuit, which can lead to book contracts and lucrative speaking engagements. Strong incentives are created to replace thoughtful analysis with glib sound bites. In theory, accepting fees from speaking engagements, which are often with industry groups or politically partisan organizations, presents a conflict of interest for journalists who may have to cover them, but the beneficiaries are usually able to fend off such ethical accusations with righteous indignation.

Fallows also charged that by presenting politics as "a depressing spectacle, rather than as a vital activity in which citizens can and should be engaged,"[3] journalists distort the American political process and undermine the vitality of our civic culture. Although citizens, when given the opportunity, ask candidates questions about important public issues, journalists too often focus on scandal or how the politicians are spinning the issue for political advantage.

Fallows was hardly alone in his views. Noam Chomsky, a long-time critic of U.S. foreign policy, turned his attention to the media in *Manufacturing Consent: The Political Economy of the Mass Media* (written with Edward Herman) and *Necessary Illusions: Thought Control in Democratic Society*. Far from being watchdogs defending our civil liberties, Chomsky charged, the mainstream news media are little more than propaganda organs for ruling elites.

The title of Robert Parry's 1992 book, *Fooling America: How Washington Insiders Twist the Truth and Manufacture the Conventional Wisdom* speaks for itself. Parry contended that the much vaunted marketplace of ideas has been replaced by an information cartel, in which only "CW" (conventional wisdom) approved ideas and information reach the general public with any frequency.[4]

In 1990, Martin Lee and Norman Solomon published *Unreliable Sources: A Guide to Detecting Bias in the News*,[5] which argues that corporate ownership of the news media results in widespread and systematic bias in the news, in favor of corporate interests, the political establishment, and its own bottom line. A similar theme has been a recurring message of *Extra!*, the magazine of media watchdog group Fairness and Accuracy in Reporting.

When Mark Hertsgaard published *On Bended Knee: The Press and the Reagan Presidency* in 1988, he accused the U.S. news media of having "abdicated its responsibility to report fully and accurately to the American people what their government was really doing."[6] But there was little response from journalism's ethics establishment. Rather, when Ralph

Barney, principal author of Chapter II of *Doing Ethics in Journalism,* addressed the matter of press criticism, he simply asserted that "the strongest critics are those who feel threatened by media disclosures or practices, those who have a vested interest in passive media."[7]

Barney clearly had not been listening to the likes of Hertsgaard, Fallows, Parry, and Chomsky, who were charging, among other things, that the press was too passive and/or servile. This response cannot be dismissed as one academic's opinion; *Doing Ethics in Journalism* is the official voice of the SPJ.

The revised code does address one of the issues raised by critics: the matter of speaking fees. After failing to reach agreement on the issue in 1995, the society did include in its revised code a provision stating that journalists "should refuse gifts, favors, fees, free travel and special treatment, and shun secondary employment, political involvement, public service and service in community organizations *if they compromise journalistic integrity*" (italics added). But it is left up to the journalists themselves to decide whether accepting speaking fees will violate their integrity.

Earlier versions of the code contained a clause that called on members to actively criticize journalists who violated the code, but these were dropped in 1987. Commented Casey Bukro, a dissenting member of the 1996 SPJ Ethics Committee: "A code that doesn't require you to do anything is soon forgotten. . . . It's gutless."[8] This may leave some people wondering about the meaning and importance of codes of ethics.

Explicit Formulations of Ethical Principles

The SPJ Code of Ethics, drawn up in 1926, received its first revision in 1973 and was revised again in 1984, 1987, and 1996.[9] In its most recent formulation, the SPJ Ethics Committee has reduced the basic principles to four:

> Seek truth and report it.
> Minimize harm.
> Act independently.
> Be accountable.[10]

The duty of journalists, according to the preamble to the SPJ Code of Ethics, is to further justice and democracy "by seeking truth and providing a fair and comprehensive account of events and issues." Earlier versions of the code called on journalists "to perform with intelligence, objectivity, accuracy and fairness," but the most recent revision drops all mention of objectivity, instead calling on journalists to "serve the public with thoroughness and honesty."

Other codes of ethics offer similar formulations. Article IV of the ASNE Statement of Principles, entitled Truth and Accuracy, asserts that: "Good faith with the reader is the foundation of good journalism. Every effort must be made to assure that the news content is accurate, free from bias and in context, and that all sides are presented fairly."

Although the "ethic of truth-telling" referred to by Ed Lambeth in the preceding chapter[11] is nowhere explicitly explained in the most prominent codes of ethics and conduct, truth is mentioned in several codes, usually in connection with accuracy. The first principle in the most recent revision of the SPJ Code is to "Seek Truth and Report It."

There is a continuing tension between an understanding of the concept of truth that equates truth and facticity, and conceptions of truth that seek "larger truths" or the "big picture." However truth may be defined, accuracy is nonetheless one of the central values of the codes, and relative to that value, what Janet Cooke did was wrong. Cooke broke faith with her readers. Her report was worse than inaccurate; it was simply untrue. But that alone is insufficient to explain the unique notoriety of the Cooke case or to distinguish it from the numerous other cases in which reporters have broken faith with their readers through false or distorted reporting.

The codes also make reference to other ethical concerns, though these are generally given less prominence. The SPJ Code calls on journalists to "avoid undercover or surreptitious methods of gathering information except when traditional open methods will not yield information vital to the public," and asserts that "use of such methods should be explained as part of the story." The right of journalists to protect the confidentiality of their sources is recognized in most codes, but several, including the ASNE Statement of Principles, insist that "unless there is a clear and pressing need to maintain confidences, sources of information should be identified." Public disclosure is emphasized in several codes, as in the SPJ Code, which pledges journalists to "recognize a special obligation to ensure that the public's business is conducted in the open, and that government records are open to inspection."

The *Washington Post*'s guidelines explicitly prohibit plagiarism and obliquely assert that claims of national interest or community interest by national or community officials do not automatically equate with the national or community interest. This latter claim presumably is intended to indicate the newspaper's right and responsibility to make independent judgments when asked to withhold or publish information "in the national interest" or in the interest of the community. A right of privacy is explicitly acknowledged only by the SPJ Code.

Problematic Aspects of the Fundamental Principles

Examined more closely, several of the central ethical principles cited above turn out to be profoundly problematic. We'll review each separately.

Conflict of Interest.   The injunction to avoid conflicts of interest means that the reporter is to maintain autonomy from his/her sources. The reality of newsgathering, however, is an inextricable interdependence between reporters and sources. This is particularly true of institutionally generated news (such as press conferences, reports of governmental agencies, police reports) that constitutes the bulk of hard news. Reporters must cultivate sources and are keenly aware that their future access to information depends on how they handle today's story. Sources, in turn, cultivate reporters. The terms of trade depend on the relative power of the parties, but neither party can make any claim to true autonomy, except in unusual circumstances. This same problem applies to the SPJ's injunction to "act independently."

Accuracy.   What is most problematic about the concept of accuracy is its ambiguous relationship to truthfulness. The vast majority of the news that reporters gather is information produced and disseminated by bureaucratic organizations. A report quoting a Pentagon spokesman on the number of casualties in the invasion of Panama can be simultaneously completely accurate as a representation of what the spokesman said, but quite inaccurate as a representation of what actually happened. Moreover, a report can be completely accurate as a representation of a particular state of affairs and at the same time misleading as a representation of a larger situation.

Objectivity.   This term is used in journalism to refer both to an epistemological concept and to a set of journalistic practices that are sometimes claimed to produce a certain kind of knowledge. Even though few reporters defend objectivity as a theoretical concept, the "objective" style of reporting continues to predominate in American journalism. Christopher Lasch, among others, has argued that the introduction into journalistic practice of the concept of objectivity, with its heavy reliance on the authority of experts, has led to a sweeping devaluation of the opinions and discourse of ordinary citizens, as well as the exclusion of the public not only from the newspaper as a public forum, but ultimately from the political process.[12]

Fairness.   Fairness can also be problematic in a variety of ways. Is it fair to report the indictment of a person who may be innocent? Does fairness require treating all points of view to a dispute as equally valid? Does fairness require that equal numbers of men and women be the authors or subjects of the stories on the front page of the *New York Times*? Is it fair for journalists themselves to be the ultimate arbiters of whether they are being fair?

Sensationalism.   The injunction to avoid sensationalism stands in stark contradiction to another fundamental reality of journalism, which is that sensationalism is built into the concept of news. Prevailing conceptions of the newsworthy place a high value on the coverage of dramatic departures from the ordinary and on the presentation of events in as emotionally compelling a way as possible.

A Conceptual Hierarchy

There is a hierarchy to journalism's ethical system. Although the various components of this system were created at different times and for varying purposes, it is possible to identify a conceptual hierarchy with different levels of abstraction. At the most abstract level, there is a fundamental conception of the responsibility of the news media (to provide the public with vital information), which is translated into a set of ethical principles (for example, the directive to avoid conflict of interest). These principles are in turn translated into operational rules of procedure (for instance, refusing to take gifts from news sources), and the rules of procedure are in turn subject to interpretation (does a cup of coffee count?) and enforcement (what is the appropriate sanction?). Each of the points of translation is also, at least potentially, a point of conflict.

What is interesting is how, in practice, one moves from one level to the other. Although the relationship between these levels of abstraction is represented as one of logical entailment, one may fairly ask, why these translations? Why does the conception of the responsibility of the news media translate into ethical principles about accuracy and conflict of interest, but not into ethical principles about the allocation of resources or (in most cases) guarantees of public access? Why are these ethical principles (like avoiding conflict of interest) translated into procedural rules that govern the conduct of employees, but not into rules governing the economic relationships that corporate media entities may enter into?

When journalistic actions are categorized as unethical within this system, that judgment is made relative to these procedural rules rather than to a broader conception of the social responsibility of the press. There are occasional instances where a news medium is criticized directly for failing to give its audience the news they need in order to participate actively in self-governance (for example, *USA Today* is frequently criticized for superficiality), but by and large these criticisms are not taken as ethical criticisms within the journalism community. Rather, they are seen as issues of quality.

Two questions now arise: Where do the internal tensions at the heart of journalism's central ethical principles come from, and how are they resolved at the level of procedural rules?

Applying the Rules

First, how are the fundamental principles cited above translated into procedural rules?

Fairness.   The principle of fairness, when translated into rules of procedure, means that when questions of wrong-doing are at issue, reporters must attempt to determine the truth of the allegations and give the accused the opportunity to reply. When the issue at hand is a matter of public controversy, the principle of fairness means that all points of view must be represented. "Persons publicly accused should be given the earliest opportunity to respond," says the ASNE Statement of Principles.[13] "Every effort should be made to present all sides of controversial issues," states the *Chicago Sun-Times* Code of Professional Standards.[14]

The *Washington Post* Standards and Ethics assert that "Fairness results from a few simple practices: No story is fair if it omits facts of major importance or significance . . . ; includes essentially irrelevant information at the expense of significant facts . . . ; consciously or unconsciously misleads or deceives the reader . . . ; [or] if reporters hide their biases or emotions behind such subtly pejorative words as 'refused,' 'despite,' 'admit,' and 'massive.'"[15] Notably, the *Post* does not explicitly affirm a right of reply for subjects of news stories who feel that they have been unfairly treated.

This definition resolves the problematic character of the concept of journalistic fairness by narrowing the scope of the concept. Within the institutionalized discourse of journalism ethics, that scope does not extend to such questions as whether it is fair that the front page of the *New York Times* is dominated by stories by or about men or even to such American journalistic practices as publishing the details of charges against persons accused of crimes—a practice that is illegal in some other countries because of the damage that it may do to innocent persons.

Accuracy. The principle of accuracy means that news media have an obligation to ascertain the correctness of the facts they publish. "Every effort will be made to avoid errors or inaccuracies. There is no excuse for failure to check a fact or allegation" (*Chicago Sun-Times* Code). "This newspaper is pledged to minimize errors and to correct them when they occur" (*Washington Post* Standards).[16]

Although most of the codes principally deal with inaccuracy as involving misstatement of fact, some, like the SPJ Code, also address other forms of misrepresentation. The SPJ Code insists that "headlines, news teases and promotional material, photos, video, audio, graphics, sound bites and quotations do not misrepresent. They should not oversimplify or highlight incidents out of context." By defining the duty of accuracy in terms of misstatements of fact, this procedural rule resolves the problematic character of the duty of accuracy. As long as the information is attributed (even if it is attributed to an anonymous source), the reporter is responsible for the accuracy of the quote, but not its propositional content.

Objectivity. In practice, the potentially troublesome character of the concept of objectivity is neutralized by equating objectivity with facts, sharply distinguished from opinions and value judgments. Virtually all of the codes implicitly or explicitly acknowledge this distinction. "Sound practice . . . demands a clear distinction for the reader between news reports and opinion. Articles that contain opinion or personal interpretation should be clearly identified," asserts the ASNE Statement. Here's how it is expressed in the *Washington Post* Standards:

On this newspaper the separation of news columns from the Editorial Page and the Op-Ed Page is solemn and complete. This separation is intended to serve the reader, who is entitled to facts on the news pages and to opinions on the Editorial and Op-Ed pages. But nothing in this separation of functions and powers is intended to eliminate from the news columns honest, in depth reporting, or analysis or commentary, when such departures from strictly factual reporting are plainly labeled.[17]

Until the most recent revision, objectivity was explicitly embraced by the SPJ Code, which asserted that "Objectivity in reporting the news . . . is a standard of performance towards which we strive. We honor those who achieve it." The *Washington Post* Standards acknowledge that "arguments about objectivity are endless" and urges fairness as a more meaningful standard. But even in codes of ethics that do not discuss objectivity explicitly, the fact/opinion distinction is explicitly acknowledged, as in the following statement from the *Chicago Sun-Times* Code: "Articles of opinion and analysis shall be properly labeled as such and kept distinctive from news coverage."[18]

Conflict of Interest.   In practice, the admonition to avoid conflict of interest means that reporters are not to accept gifts, special treatment, or privileges that might compromise their integrity or to enter into political, personal, or financial relationships that might compromise their credibility or objectivity. Most codes also restrict secondary employment and other financial relationships with actual or potential news sources. "Remain free of associations and activities that may compromise integrity or damage credibility," says the SPJ Code. "Refuse gifts, favors, fees, free travel and special treatment, and shun secondary employment, political involvement, public office, and service in community organizations if they compromise journalistic integrity."[19]

In 1981, the *Detroit Free Press* issued a very detailed statement of policy on conflict of interest. Journalists were admonished to remember that gifts of value are to be returned to the donor or donated to charity, with an explanatory note to the donor; free tickets are prohibited, but reporters and photographers may make use of press boxes and press rooms where those are provided; staff members may not enter into business relationships with news sources or invest in businesses that present potential for conflict of interest, and they should avoid making news judgments about companies in which they have investments.

Defining conflict of interest in this way simply conceals the fundamental interdependencies between reporters and sources. The most valuable gifts that reporters and sources can exchange—scoops and favorable coverage—simply aren't recognized by the definition. Moreover, defining conflict of interest strictly in terms of the conduct of individual journalists removes from the arena of moral judgment the often much more serious conflicts of interest that can arise at the level of the institution: conflicts of interest between the institution's economic and political interests and its obligations of service to the community.

Sensationalism. The admonition to avoid sensationalism is generally translated to mean that journalists must keep their reporting within the boundaries of community standards of good taste. In the words of the SPJ Code, "Show good taste. Avoid pandering to morbid curiosity."

In practice, the existence of tabloid newspapers (the *National Enquirer*, the *New York Post*) and tabloid news programs (*Hard Copy, Inside Edition*) gives a constructive definition to sensationalism which renders a wide range of practices permissible as long as they stay within certain ill-defined and ever-shifting boundaries. Writing in the *New Republic*, William Powers describes the ease with which the strictures about sensationalism—and fairness—are circumvented by the mainstream press, and all without violating the ethical rules:

> Almost immediately [after a scandal is broken by the tabloid press], a story appears in *The Washington Post* under the byline of media reporter Howard Kurtz. . . . By delivering the scandal as a media story, Kurtz launders the news itself for mainstream resale. Generally, the *Post* and its peers consider stories about the trysting habits of politicians and entertainers far too downmarket for their news columns. But when one of these stories arrives in the frame of a chin-scratcher about media ethics, it's perfectly respectable.[20]

Why These Rules?

Generally, the codes of ethics offer two sorts of rationales for these rules: one asserts that these policies are necessary to safeguard the mission of the press, while the other asserts that these policies are necessary to safeguard the credibility of the press. This duality reflects a broader ambiguity about the role of ethics in journalism. Is its principal function to ensure that the press fulfills its responsibility to the public, or is its principal function to protect the image and thus the interests of the press? This ambiguity may suggest what is at least a factor in Cooke's unique notoriety: Although the harm produced by her trespass may be minor in terms of the public interest, the context in which it occurred, a Pulitzer Prize, made it a major trespass in terms of undermining the credibility of the press.

Although the codes generally begin with preambles about the mission of the press, the prescriptions of the codes are largely negative, specifying prohibited conduct and defining the limits of the permissible, rather than defining journalistic excellence or priorities. In fact, as the term ethics is used in journalistic discourse, it generally occurs in connection with misconduct. There is a discourse of excellence in journalism, signaled through a system of prizes and other honors, whose values sometimes come into conflict with those of journalism's ethical codes. Thus "great" newspaper photographs are almost by definition photographs that are emotionally compelling because of the degree to which they reveal private emotions, a degree that may bring them into conflict with journalistic norms concerning privacy.

The Philosophical Rationale: The Social Responsibility of the Press

Theories of the mission of the press have evolved with the changing role of the press in society. In an influential book published in 1956, press theorist Wilbur Schramm and several colleagues claimed to identify four competing theories of the press, including authoritarian, Soviet communist (a modification of the authoritarian model), libertarian, and social responsibility (a modification of the libertarian model).[21]

The social responsibility theory was given prominence by the 1947 report *A Free and Responsible Press*, issued by the Commission on Freedom of the Press, better known as the Hutchins Commission, after its chairman, Robert Hutchins.[22] At present, there is wide, but not universal, acceptance in the journalism community of the social responsibility theory of the press as the conceptual foundation of the ethical principles listed above. The central idea is that the news media have a responsibility to the society as a whole: to provide the public with the information that they need in order to function as active participants in a democracy. This idea is often referred to as the "vital information" premise.

First among the responsibilities identified by the commission was the responsibility to provide "an accurate and comprehensive account of the day's news"; other responsibilities included providing a forum ("marketplace") for the exchange of ideas of individuals and social groups, and providing a vehicle for expressing and clarifying the values of the society. Linked to this theory of the role of the press is a commitment to a correspondence theory of truth, which gives a central role to the concept of objectivity. In order to fulfill their obligations as citizens in a democracy, cit-

izens must have a reliable picture of the world and of the days' events—
that is, a picture that corresponds to the facts. This conception of the role
of the news media provides the theoretical foundation for the ethical principles of journalism ethics. Distorting that picture of the world—through
inaccuracy, sensationalism, or bias—is direct malfeasance; entering into
relationships that might create conflict of interest is wrong because it may
lead to distortion.

But if the ultimate basis for the emphasis on accuracy is a concern for
giving the citizen an accurate picture of the world that can serve as the basis for active participation in public life, then the singular notoriety of the
Cooke case seems even more mysterious than before. Surely there are
more significant cases of failures to serve that public interest.

What Gets Lost in Translation?

Within the framework of social responsibility theory, the rules of ethical
conduct articulated by the codes and the more specific procedures insti-
tuted by news organizations serve mediating functions: The codes' ethical
rules transform issues of principle based on a conception of the mission of
the press into a set of ethical norms, and the news organizations' guidelines translate those norms into operational rules. Philip Meyer, a professor of journalism at the University of North Carolina and a prominent
scholar in the field, argues that news media can audit their ethical standards generally through quantified measurements of the accuracy of their
reporting, a notion that indicates the importance of the mediating function played by rules:

> In focusing on accuracy as an indicator of overall ethical stance, a newspa-
> per—or an outside observer for that matter—would be engaging in what so-
> cial scientists call "operationalization." To operationalize is to move from the
> large and the abstract to the specific and the measurable. The concept of
> "morality" is big, complicated, and incapable of being measured. Source per-
> ceived accuracy is a small outcropping of that concept, but it is related to the
> total concept and can be measured.[23]

Note that there are two stages of translation involved in Meyer's suggestion—from the broad notion of morality to the more narrowly defined
concept of accuracy, and from the concept of accuracy to the yet more restrictive concept of "source perceived accuracy." "Source perceived accuracy" means that the news medium can get a measure of the quality of its

reporting by going back to the sources of its information and asking whether the published or broadcast report accurately reflects what the sources said.

The practical consequence of using this narrow conception of accuracy as a monitor of overall ethical performance is that a news medium which, for example, restricted its coverage of the Gulf War to reprinting verbatim the official statements of Defense Department spokesmen would not have to concern itself with whether anything the spokesmen said was actually true nor with whether those statements, even if true in their particular assertions, might misrepresent the larger picture. Rather, they need only concern themselves with whether the spokesmen believe that they have been quoted accurately.

Of course, Meyer doesn't really intend to equate source perceived accuracy with morality or even accuracy, but only to suggest that the former can serve as a barometer of overall ethical performance. Journalists who are scrupulous about the accuracy with which they quote Defense Department spokesmen will presumably be equally scrupulous in their commitment to reporting all sides fairly.

Another example of the mediating function played by procedural rules can be found in a 1980 case involving the *Spokane Chronicle*. In order to assist police in the apprehension of a rapist, the newspaper withheld information from the public and published a report that was at least misleading, if not actually false. Spokane's rival newspaper, the *Spokesman-Review,* published a report charging that the *Chronicle* reporter had "worked for hours" with a police detective to make the story sound as if another suspected rapist were the prime suspect in the case in question. The *Chronicle* reporter defended himself against the implicit charge of unethical conduct by appealing to an ethical norm for justification: "I did not take turns at the typewriter with the detective, as [the *Spokesman-Review* reporter] suggested, but carefully reviewed details with him in the interest of accuracy."[24]

Thus, questions of principle (Did the newspaper violate its responsibility to disclose the whole truth in appropriate context? Did the newspaper cross the line from objective detachment to participation?) are translated into questions of procedure (Did the detective actually help the reporter write his story? Was the story accurate?). But that process of translation, shaped by the dynamics of power within the institution, is problematic: How well, in fact, do these procedural rules insure that the press will fulfill its social responsibility? Does something get lost in translation?

A Case Study: The Marketplace of Ideas

As a case in point, consider what happens to one of the core values identified by the Hutchins Commission—the concept that the news media have
a duty to serve as a "marketplace of ideas"—as it moves across the gradient from general statement of mission to abstract principles to rules of
procedure. Although the lines are not clear-cut, it is possible to identify
varying levels of theoretical abstraction in the expression of ethical principles: the theoretical work of the Hutchins Commission, dealing with the
role of the media in society, is the most abstract; the codes of ethics of professional organizations are intermediate; and the policy and practice statements of the individual news media are the most specific and least theoretical.

At different points along this gradient, the relative importance placed
on different ethical values shifts. Although among the principal concerns
of the Hutchins Commission was the preservation of the marketplace of
ideas and guaranteeing the public's access to the media for the expression
of a diversity of ideas, and especially unpopular ideas, this value receives
relatively little attention in the professional and institutional codes.

The *Washington Post* Standards prominently acknowledge as first
among the media's special responsibilities a duty to "listen to the voiceless," but not a duty to "be a voice for the voiceless." The ASNE Statement
also makes passing reference to the right of free expression "guarantee[d]
to the people through their press" and of the function of the press as a "forum for debate," but gives no explicit acknowledgment of a right of public
access.

The *Chicago Sun-Times* Code does recognize "the right of the public to
comment on public issues or material appearing in our pages." The code
further pledges that every edition will provide a department for such commentary and correction, "subject only to limitations of relevancy and
space."

Previous versions of the SPJ Code upheld the right of journalists "to
speak unpopular opinions and the privilege to agree with the majority,"
but that right has disappeared from the 1996 Code. The newest version
does urge journalists to "give voice to the voiceless; official and unofficial
sources of information can be equally valid"; and to "support the open exchange of views, even views they find repugnant." Under the heading, "Be
Accountable," the code asserts that "Journalists are accountable to their
readers, listeners, viewers, and each other." Journalists are told to "clarify

and explain news coverage and invite dialogue with the public over journalistic conduct" and to "encourage the public to voice grievances against
the news media." But this falls far short of a right of public access or even a
right to a published response for aggrieved parties.

If there is a decreasing emphasis on the marketplace of ideas as we move
from the most theoretical formulations of missions to the more concrete
formulations of ethical principles, there is a similar and further de-
emphasis on the marketplace of ideas as we move from the realm of theory to particular cases. The examination of cases that are problematized as
unethical in practice reveals few if any that can be categorized as "failure to
promote a marketplace of ideas." Newspapers provide a very limited forum for the expression of the viewpoints of ordinary citizens in the
columns of letters to the editor, but no similar forum exists in commercial
television, which has long since superseded newspapers as the primary
news medium in this society. During the era of the Fairness Doctrine,
some television stations aired guest editorials on topics of current concern, but even that very limited practice has disappeared.

Similarly, the obligation of the news media to provide "an accurate and
comprehensive account of the day's news," which is acknowledged in the
most abstract formulations, disappears at the level of the more specific
and concrete codes and especially at the level of practice. In practice, while
some newspapers may still make an effort to fulfill the ill-defined ideal of
"comprehensive" coverage, such an ideal has long since disappeared (if it
ever existed) in local television news.

The Ideological Function of Journalistic Principles

The function of journalism's fundamental principles is ideological in the
sense of the term described by Dorothy Smith:

> Ideology as contrasted with knowledge identifies . . . the interested proce-
> dures which people use as a means not to know. . . . It is a practice which has
> the effect of making the fundamental features of our own society mysterious
> because it prevents us from seeing them as problematic. The concept be-
> comes a substitute for reality. It becomes a boundary, or a terminus through
> which inquiry cannot proceed. What ought to be explained is treated as fact
> or as assumption.[25]

In other words, a principle is ideological if its function is not to explain,
but rather to foreclose inquiry. Each of journalism's principles can be un-

derstood as ideological in that sense: They resolve fundamental tensions in journalistic practice by defining the problem in a way that avoids conflict with institutional interests.

The Translation Effect

A closer examination of how the most basic notions about the mission of the press are translated into ethical principles and how those principles are translated into rules of procedure reveals a systematic pattern to what is lost in translation: Each of these translations serves to resolve an internal contradiction. In some cases, the contradiction is between the news media's stated mission of public service and its institutional character as a profit-making enterprise, while in other cases it is a contradiction between journalistic principle and journalistic practice.

Most broadly, what is filtered out in the process of translation are those issues that could present a challenge to the prerogatives of ownership (and particularly the pursuit of profits) or to the institutional interests of the medium. Thus, although the publisher's activities on behalf of the governor may seem to involve the newspaper in a conflict of interest, as conflict of interest is defined within journalism ethics (in so far as it is defined at all), it pertains to the conduct of journalists but not to the conduct of publishers.

Similarly, the principles pertaining to fairness and objectivity are not translated into procedural rules regarding how resources are to be allocated. An editor's decisions about the number of reporters and editors or the number of column inches that will be given to sports coverage versus political coverage simply are not acknowledged as ethical issues. Although there are many journalists who believe that abolishing the agriculture beat and creating a new section devoted to shopping reflects regrettable priorities, there are probably few who would be inclined to label those decisions as unethical. In part, that reluctance reflects a respect for common usage; it isn't the sort of thing that usually gets labeled as unethical. At the same time, that reluctance reflects the material circumstances in which the internal discourse about ethics takes place. Employees question the ethics of their bosses at their peril.

Traditionally, there has been a generally accepted ethical rule (curiously absent from most of the formal codes of ethics) that dictates a wall of separation between editorial and advertising—there is to be no interference with the editorial process by either the advertising department or the advertisers themselves, and the selection and editing of news stories is to be totally independent of any consideration of the economic interests of the news medium. But that rule is applied only at the level of the story. The creation of entire sections (such as food, homes, motoring, and travel) with an editorial content chosen to attract particular kinds of advertising is not regarded as a breach in the wall.

The wall is also circumvented by another strategy. Increasingly, newspaper advertising departments are putting out themed "advertorial" sections, which look like editorial sections and are identified as advertising only by the words "advertising supplement" in small type. Because they are identified as advertising, they are not held to the same standards as the editorial content of the paper. Another variant on this strategy is the "branded product" section devoted to topics such as travel or fashion, (such as the *New York Times' Sophisticated Traveler*), which is produced by the newsroom staff, but which as a matter of policy does not carry negative, critical, or watchdog stories.

These strategies suggest an important but seldom discussed function of the ethical rules: by defining a class of proscribed practices, they serve to legitimate the larger class of practices that are not proscribed. The concern about the television anchor who posed for *Playboy* is part of a broader concern about the credibility of women in television. Her actions encourage viewers to regard women in television news as sex objects rather than as news reporters. But again, why is it in this specific case that the exploitation of female sexuality is treated as ethically problematic? It is an unwritten rule that only physically attractive women can be employed as news anchors, and it is universally understood that their physical attributes and personality are used to "sell" the program to its audience. This universal practice is almost never challenged as unethical.

There are a number of component factors that make the individual reporter a more likely target than the broader institution. One is that television is recognized as having an economic imperative that legitimates certain forms of sexual exploitation. In support of this imperative, a set of rules about the limits of this exploitation have emerged, which by defining the impermissible (that is, female television anchors who project a cheap or unconstrained sexuality) also defines the field for the permissible exploitation of female sexuality.

Power and the Institutionalized Ethical Discourse

At what level and in which cases will principles such as fairness, objectivity, and conflict of interest be applied? The answers are determined or strongly shaped by relations of power within the newsroom. In practice, as media critics have noted, the principle of fairness stops at the U.S. border. The right of Fidel Castro, Muammar Ghadafi, or Saddam Hussein to fairness, to a balanced airing of their perspective, is often not even acknowledged. When it is acknowledged, it is likely to be by way of a token paragraph, whose credibility is negated by the context within which it appears.

The principle of objectivity is typically acknowledged at the level of the individual reporter and the individual news story, but not at the level of institutional conduct. A series of reports discussing the problem of drug use in the black community can be scrupulously objective in content, but the series itself may distort public perceptions about the relative frequency of drug use in the black and white communities by the absence of similar reports about the frequency of drug use in the white community.

Some of the marginalized cases do seem to count as violations of the rules even within the institutionalized discourse, as in the case of an editor removing material from a story that might be offensive to advertisers. But even in these kinds of cases, there are several factors that make it unlikely that the case will receive wide circulation or that the editor will be subject to any form of ethical accountability.

One factor is that there is rarely anything that can be pointed to as a simple and clear-cut case of unethical conduct; rather, there is a rule that can be pointed to and the relation of the action to the rule can be contested. The outcome of the contest is likely to be a reflection of the relative power of the parties involved. In the example of the editor who deleted information about a fur protest from an article about fur fashions, although the action appears to violate a prohibition against editing stories to please advertisers, the editor could call upon other journalistic and ethical considerations in defense of those actions—an insistence that the perspective of the animal rights activists is already adequately represented in the newspaper and a prior obligation to the advertisers, who purchased space with a reasonable expectation that their advertising would not appear in a hostile editorial environment. In a further exploration of the legitimacy of each side's point of view, the feature editor's claims might prove insupportable, but the point is precisely that there is unlikely to be any further exploration.

Another factor is that rules have little meaning without sanctions. The term must be understood very broadly as including everything from the formal sanctions specified in employment contracts to the possibility of getting a dart from the *Columbia Journalism Review* or being the object of critical editorial comment in another publication.

The range of sanctions available to enforce compliance with the ethical rules is extremely variable. Reporters and editors can, generally, be disciplined through measures ranging from reprimands to suspension and termination. Those actions are, however, subject to a number of institutional and informal constraints, including (in some cases) the legal protections provided by a union contract and the force of public and newsroom opinion. Editors have the right to interrogate reporters about how they got their information, and reporters are required to answer truthfully, on penalty of disciplinary action.

At many newspapers a reporter who commits an inaccuracy deemed to warrant a formal correction is required to submit, in writing, a note explaining how and why the error occurred and is expected to offer assurances that errors of this kind will not be repeated. It is an effective means of ensuring an ongoing effort by all reporters to conform to this norm.

No comparable mechanisms of accountability exist for top managers. Although the standards theoretically apply equally to all, the degree to which managers such as executive editors or publishers can be held accountable is considerably more limited, constrained by their influence over all phases of the normative process—by their power to define the rules, to decide whether a particular case is a violation of the rules, and to bring sanctions to bear. This is not to suggest that there is no ethical accountability for editors, publishers, and owners, but only that the ethical discourse is shaped by relations of power.

In most cases, those who might wish to treat an editor's decision as unethical have neither the institutional standing that gives them the appropriate authority to act nor any significant medium for the circulation of their opinions. They are free, although not in an unproblematic sense, to discuss the decision amongst themselves, but this does not constitute a significant challenge to the legitimacy of prevailing practices. Some of the conditions necessary for the functioning of the ethical language game are missing when, for example, an editor may simply refuse to acknowledge that he or she is accountable to this audience on these issues. Where there are no sanctions, there can be no accountability. The degree of accountability to which journalists are held in actual practice varies with the power of editors, colleagues, news subjects, and members of the public to call them to account.

Journalists may have great difficulty talking coherently about theoretical questions of journalism ethics, but few lack a clear understanding of how the institutionalized discourse operates. In another essay in the SPJ report titled "For Journalists, Inescapable Impact of Ethics," Manuel Galvan, chairman of SPJ's Ethics Committee, offers a good illustration of the use of ethical discourse as defensive strategy: "When do you feel secure with a decision?" Galvan asks rhetorically. "When you can defend your action to the person you are writing about, to your colleagues and that journalism prof you had, you're getting there. It's a desired state, similar to the definition of a good city editor as being someone who is right or wrong, but always certain."[26]

The essay by Galvan and the essay cited earlier by Johnson agree on one basic point, "the bottom line is to make sure that you're [sic] personal ethics can't be questioned." In other words, "Am I going to get into trouble?" This formulation expresses in a very direct way the role of power relationships in shaping the ethical priorities of journalism. If journalists equate acting ethically with "being able to defend your actions to the person you are writing about, your colleagues, and that journalism prof you had," rather than with either intrinsic principles or some concept of consequences for the common good, then journalism ethics becomes (in Gaye Tuchman's terms) "a defensive ritual" rather than a genuine variety of moral discourse. This raises an important question: By what means can the institutionalized discourse be transformed so that issues not previously recognized as ethical gain such recognition?

Codes of ethics, and the conversation that surrounds them, are supposed to be tools that not only guide journalists but also safeguard their mission. When publishers pressure journalists to favor advertisers, or when organized interests within the community threaten retaliation for coverage that displeases them, the journalist has a set of professional norms that she can appeal to in justification and as the basis of a moral claim on the support of other professionals. But when the codes of ethics and the conversation that surrounds them are focused on the wrong issues, they lose their capacity to protect the journalist or safeguard her mission. The wholesale abandonment of routine coverage of the operations of local government by television and newspapers around the country was made possible, at least in part, by the fact that these trends were not categorized as ethically significant.

Power relations in journalism are not static. The balance of power—between reporters and editors, between journalists and owners, and between political and economic interests—has been continuously transformed throughout the history of American journalism. The roots of the Janet Cooke case lie buried deep in that history.

3

Contemporary Ethical Concepts in Historical Context

Ethics talk has a long history in American journalism. The vocabulary of ethics has been invoked by editors and publishers since Colonial times to attack their economic rivals or to defend themselves against their critics. But for ethics talk to be more than just talk, journalists must be able to operate with autonomy and accountability. Autonomy means the freedom to act according to the dictates of one's conscience and professional judgment; accountability means that there is some mechanism in place to insure that one fulfills one's responsibilities or to impose sanctions when one fails to fulfill them. The degree of autonomy and accountability that American journalists have had has varied greatly throughout our history.

According to one widely held view, the history of journalism ethics reflects the march of moral progress: a gradually increasing awareness by journalists of their professional responsibilities and a parallel development of the institutional framework for assuring a high standard of journalistic conduct. This progress can be seen in the growing professionalism of the workforce (increasing autonomy) and in the development of formal standards of journalistic conduct (increasing accountability). Though there have been occasional lapses and reverses, the improved ethical character of contemporary journalism can be seen in the separation of news from opinion (dictated by the standard of objectivity) and in the separation of the news and business functions of the newspaper, which prevents advertisers or the economic interests of the newspaper itself from interfering with the newspaper's fulfillment of its responsibility to its public.[1]

This view is rejected by a number of press critics such as Lance Bennett, who has argued that

Journalism, like most professions, developed a set of business practices first, then endowed those practices with a set of impressive professional rationalizations, and finally proceeded to rewrite its history in ways that made the practices seem to emerge, as if through immaculate conception, from an inspiring set of professional ideals.[2]

Throughout the history of American journalism, the focus of ethics talk has usually been closely linked to the economic interests of the press.

Although there have been craft norms in journalism for as long as there have been journalists, the emergence of standards self-consciously referred to as ethical is a relatively recent development. The earliest reference to a code of ethics for journalists appeared in the 1840s, and the first known example of press criticism that made explicit reference to journalistic ethics was published in 1889.[3] The first formal code of ethics did not appear until 1911.

The Early Partisan Press and Impartiality

During the era of the partisan press, there were debates over impartiality that foreshadowed more recent debates over objectivity. The demand for impartiality was not expressed as a demand that newspapers limit themselves to "just the facts," but rather as a demand that more than one interpretation be presented. "By impartiality," wrote a New York printer in 1799, "we mean the method which they adhere to in editing their papers; instead of Printing only in favor of one nation, they publish as they receive the information, both against France and Great Britain: this conduct discovers the real American."[4]

Impartiality had seemed an important principle in the Revolutionary period, when American journalists fought against the censorship imposed by British colonial authorities. But in an era when newspapers were heavily dependent on patronage from political parties, American journalists lacked the autonomy to embrace this value; their accountability was to their patrons, rather than the public at large. Hazel Dicken-Garcia cites a New Jersey printer's 1798 rejection of impartiality:

The times demand decision; there is a right and a wrong, and the printer, who under the specious name of impartiality jumbles both truth and falsehood into the same paper is either doubtful of his own judgment in determining truth from falsehood or is governed by ulterior motives.[5]

By the 1840s, with the emergence of the penny press, partisanism had become one of the main targets of ethics talk in journalism. Because they were economically dependent on advertisers rather than on political parties, the publishers of the new penny papers were able to take a stance of greater political neutrality and, from that standpoint, to make partisanism an ethical issue.

The publishers of the penny press were, however, much less interested in exploring the ethical implications of their own advertising policies. Michael Schudson quotes from the October 11, 1837, edition of the *Boston Daily Times*:

> Some of our readers complain of the great number of patent medicines advertised in this paper. To this complaint we can only reply that it is for our interest to insert such advertisements as are not indecent or improper in their language, without any inquiry whether the articles advertised are what they purport to be. That is an inquiry for the reader who feels interested in the matter, and not for us, to make. . . . One man has as good a right as another to have his wares, his goods, his panaceas, his profession, published to the world in a newspaper, provided he pays for it.[6]

"All the penny papers, to greater or lesser degrees, adopted the language and morality of laissez-faire," reports Schudson.[7] J. Herbert Altschull cites an even blunter response to a reader's complaint about an advertiser, given by James Gordon Bennett of the *New York Herald Tribune* in 1836: "Send us more advertisements than Dr. Brandeth does—give us higher prices— we'll cut Dr. Brandeth dead—or at least curtail his space. Business is business—money is money . . . we permit no blockhead to interfere with our business."[8]

Although the lack of accountability is deplorable, the candor is refreshing. Few editors today would refer to their critics as blockheads and when challenged on the subject of objectionable advertising, most would be more likely to fall back on a ritual invocation of the First Amendment, rather than seriously engage the underlying issues of social responsibility and conflicting values.

Ethics talk was a useful weapon for both sides in the early newspaper wars. The six-penny papers waged a "moral war" (as it was then called) against James Gordon Bennett's *New York Herald* from 1840 to 1844, charging the *Herald* with indecency, blasphemy, blackmail, lying, and libel.

The Post–Civil War Press and Sensationalism

The dominant theme of ethical discourse about journalism in the years after the Civil War were sensationalism and immorality. One critic, writing in 1882, charged that the newspapers of the day had abandoned "all distinctions between wholesome, necessary intelligence" and had become "habitually guilty of indecent exposure of transactions and behavior from which healthy souls shrink in disgust and abhorrence."[9]

The emergence of sensationalism as an ethical issue was a byproduct of the trend in the post-war years towards the "story" model of journalism. Facts remained central, but the facts were to be organized in a way that made them compelling to the reader. Dicken-Garcia suggests that the Civil War played a key role in the emergence of the story model: The war had triggered the rapid expansion of the newspaper industry and given rise to an audience accustomed to dramatic accounts in the newspaper. The war generated its own drama; when the war ended, the apparatus of news consumption and production could only be sustained by the manufacture of drama.

In 1878, Joseph Pulitzer purchased the *St. Louis Post and Dispatch* and boosted circulation by emphasizing screaming headlines and political exposés. Five years later, Pulitzer took over the *New York World* and by the fall of 1886 raised its circulation from 15,000 to 250,000. The two key elements in the success of the *World* were its penny price, in a market where other newspapers (themselves the "penny press" of an earlier era) now charged two, three, or four cents a copy, and its sensationalistic style.

The newspapers of Joseph Pulitzer and William Randolph Hearst constituted a "new journalism," which represented a serious economic challenge to the established newspapers. Predictably, the established press fought back with both economic weapons (price cutting) and the discourse of morality. Leading the attack was the *New York Times*. In 1896, Adolph Ochs took over the *Times* and announced his intention to "conduct a high-standard newspaper, clean, dignified and trustworthy." "High standards" were the selling point of the new *Times*, which adopted as its slogans "All the News That's Fit to Print" and "It Does Not Soil the Breakfast Table." The next year, the *Times* joined two other more traditional newspapers in waging a new "moral war" against the *World* and Hearst's *Journal*. In a two-page story on "New Journalism and Vice," the *Times* quoted a certain Rev. Dr. W.H.P. Faunce, speaking on the occasion of the twenty-fifth anniversary of the New York Society for the Suppression of Vice:

> The press of this country to-day is engaged in a fearful struggle, one class against another. On one side stand the reputable papers which represent decency and truth, and on the other, is what calls itself the new journalism, but which is in reality as old as sin itself.[10]

What the *New York Times* sold its readers, beyond information, was respectability, understood as identification with the values of the upper classes. It did this quite self-consciously: "To be seen reading the *New York Times* is a stamp of respectability," the *Times* proclaimed in an 1898 circulation drive.[11]

The Call to Order and the Rule of Objectivity

If ethics talk was mostly cheap talk in the nineteenth century, there were signs at the beginning of the twentieth century that the conditions necessary for a meaningful conversation about journalism's responsibilities were beginning to come into place. Leading figures in journalism, such as Pulitzer and later Walter Lippmann, embraced the idea of professionalism, which carried the promise of greater autonomy and accountability for the working journalist. At the same time, newspapers began increasingly to address their readers as part of a public. Pulitzer, Hearst, and other publishers such as E. W. Scripps popularized a crusading style of journalism that made their newspapers and their readers active participants in political life. In an era when even a mid-sized American city typically had at least half a dozen newspapers competing for readers, the marketplace itself helped to create accountability.

If respectability was a weapon in the newspaper wars, Pulitzer was not about to cede the field to the *New York Times.* He donated $2 million to endow the Columbia School of Journalism, announcing, "I wish to begin a movement that will raise journalism to the rank of a learned profession, growing in the respect of the community as other professions far less important to the public interest have grown."[12]

But aspirations to respectability were not the only motive for professionalization. The last decade of the nineteenth century and the first three decades of the twentieth were a period of extreme social conflict in the United States and a high point of American radicalism. This was the era of the Haymarket riots, the Pullman massacre, the Industrial Workers of the World, Eugene Debs, and the Socialist Party. A wave of working class immigrants brought with them radical political cultures—notably socialism and anarchism, as well as militant political and labor movements, and a radical press, both immigrant and English-language.

The reaction to this militancy was a brutal reassertion of power by the most powerful elements in the society, in the form of massacres, jailings, deportations, and the closing of newspapers. Many American radicals were rounded up and imprisoned during the Palmer raids of the early 1920s.

There was also a perceived need for a reassertion of authority in the newsroom. According to James Carey, then dean of the School of Communications at the University of Illinois,

> The impulse to ethics in journalism, and in journalism education, was less a high-minded sense of the republic, than the need to assert social control over the reporter, to deflect trade unions, and to make working-class journalists into sober, responsible working men and women who would not question the prerogatives of ownership and management. . . . The development of journalism ethics was often an attack on the style of the bohemian reporter and the sensational styles and interests of the working class and the immigrant. In this sense ethics reflected status and class conflict between middle class owners and readers and working class reporters rather than a high-minded attempt to articulate a satisfying moral code.[13]

The embrace of objectivity—a term unknown before World War I—was not rooted in a naive realism, Schudson insists, but rather in its opposite. The success of government-orchestrated wartime propaganda and the growth of the great propaganda machinery of public relations coincided with the collapse of the moral universe occasioned by the Great War. All served to undermine the naive faith in facts that previously prevailed and to produce for the press a "crisis of legitimacy."

The credibility and ethical standards of journalists came under attack in works such as Upton Sinclair's *The Brass Check*, which argued that journalism had prostituted itself to the interests of Big Business.[14] This crisis of credibility and the aspiration of journalists for recognition as professionals led in the 1920s to the proliferation of schools of journalism at American universities and the formulation of numerous codes of ethics.

An understanding developed that facts were subject to interpretation and that interpretation was always subjective. The result was a hunger for some source of certainty, and Walter Lippmann was one of the early advocates of what he called objectivism, the application of the scientific method to both journalism and the collection of public information (for example, by government agencies). "As our minds become more deeply aware of their own subjectivism, we find a zest in objectivism that is not otherwise there."[15] Implicit was the notion that it was possible, through the application of scientific method, to offer an interpretation of the facts that was not itself subjective, but was guided by some universal methodological principles. "There is but one kind of unity possible in a universe as diverse as ours. It is the unity of method, rather than of aim; the unity of the disciplined experiment."[16]

There was also, in the period after World War I, a growing pessimism about the viability of participatory democracy. Lippmann was one of the leading doubters; in a series of very influential books, including *Drift and Mastery*, *Public Opinion*, and *The Phantom Public*, he argued that the public was not capable of governing itself. It was a mistake to see any special wisdom in the will of the majority and unrealistic to expect that the general public could be brought to the level of understanding necessary to make the decisions of government. Those decisions must be made by experts, guided by the spirit of scientific inquiry. As Lippmann put it, "the common interests very largely elude public opinion entirely, and can be managed only by a specialized class whose personal interests reach beyond the locality." The role of journalism, within this conception of how society should function, was the transmission of expert opinion to the public, so that the public could ratify expert decisions, a process that Lippmann labeled "the manufacture of consent."[17] Lippmann was contemptuous of public debate, viewing debate as something people do when they don't have the facts.

Professionalism, Objectivity, and Power

One way of understanding the emergence of the concepts of objectivity and professionalism is as the translation of property rights into social power. The norm of professionalism provided a restraint—never completely effective—on who could be a producer of news, and the norm of objectivity further constrained what journalists could report and who could serve as a legitimate source of news. Prior to the rise of professionalism, facts were regarded as, at least in theory, accessible to any competent observer, but the new standard imposed tighter restrictions regarding whose accounts were to be treated as credible. Similarly, although the conventions of journalism prior to the rise of objectivity required news reporting to be grounded in facts, muckraking journalists and newspapers could—and did—use facts as weapons in journalistic crusades.

The hierarchically controlled implementation and enforcement of the procedural rules of objectivity ultimately had the consequence that the autonomy of the journalist and the access of the public were restricted in favor of an expert discourse. This led to the virtual disappearance of the crusading newspaper, as newspapers increasingly became a vehicle for the dissemination of expert opinion. This was the role that Lippmann saw for the press, but its social consequence, as Christopher Lasch points out, was a delegitimation of public discourse:

> Lippmann's distrust of public opinion rested on the epistemological distinction between truth and mere opinion. Truth, as he conceived it, grew out of disinterested scientific inquiry; everything else was ideology. The scope of public debate, therefore, had to be severely restricted. . . . Ideally, public debate would not take place at all; decisions would be based on scientific "standards of measurement" alone.[18]

These consequences can be seen as part of a countermovement to the extension of formal political rights that occurred in the second half of the nineteenth century and early twentieth century which included Emancipation, women's suffrage, direct election of the Senate, and other extensions of the electoral franchise.

The idea of professionalism also invited journalists to think of themselves as belonging to the same social class and having the same class interests as their employers, rather than identifying with the rest of the newspaper's workforce. The substantial differences in social circumstances between journalists and professionals such as physicians and attorneys is obscured in the rhetoric of journalistic professionalism. Although the status of doctors and lawyers has increasingly come to resemble that of journalists, in the sense that they too are now for the most part employees of large corporations and experiencing a similar loss of professional autonomy, at the time of the formation of the codes of journalistic responsibility the degree of autonomy with which doctors and lawyers operated was far greater than that of journalists. What defined doctors and lawyers as professionals was the fact that their accountability was directly to the public.

Arguments continue to this day over whether journalism is, can be, or even should be, a profession. There is little agreement on the definition of the term, but Bernard Barber has suggested that there are four defining differences that distinguish professions:

> a high degree of generalized and systematic knowledge; primary orientation to the community interest rather than to individual self-interest; a high degree of self-control of behavior through codes of ethics internalized in the process of work socialization and through voluntary associations organized and operated by the work specialists themselves; and a system of rewards (monetary and honorary) that is primarily a set of symbols of work achieve-

ments and thus ends in themselves, not means to some end of individual self-interest.[19]

The innovations of the 1920s were designed to give journalism at least the trappings of a profession: the establishment of voluntary associations, such as the SPJ, and the ASNE; the establishment of numerous awards and competitions for journalists; the establishment of university-based professional schools; and the promulgation of codes of ethics, such as the SPJ Code of Ethics, adopted in 1926, the ASNE Canon of Ethics, adopted in 1923, and numerous codes adopted by state journalism societies.

But the question remains, is journalism truly a profession? John Merrill, after considering Barber's criteria, argues that

> obviously, it is not, although it has some of a profession's characteristics. There is no direct relationship between the journalist and his client. There is, in journalism, no minimum entrance requirement; anybody can be a journalist who can get himself hired—experience or no experience, degree or no degree. No journalist is expected (or required) to abide by any professional ethos or code of ethics. No journalist is licensed, thereby giving the "profession" some kind of control over him. There are no professional standards commonly agreed upon, and followed, by journalists. Journalists do not share in common a "high degree of generalized and systematic knowledge." Journalists do not claim for themselves the exclusive right to practice the arts (all borrowed from other disciplines) of their trade. And finally, journalists in America do not "comprise a homogeneous community."[20]

Although the picture has changed since 1974, the status of journalists remains ambiguous. On the one hand, though it may be true that "anyone can be a journalist who can get himself hired," it is becoming increasingly difficult to get hired at a major newspaper without experience and a degree. On the other hand, even if the entrance requirements have become more rigorous, critics charge that the work itself has been "de-skilled" (see Chapter 4). In addition, although journalism's professional ethics may contain inconsistencies and incoherencies, there are core values within journalism that have long been widely accepted—and widely circumvented. Journalists may not be directly employed by the public, but traditionally many reporters do see the public as their "client." That view is being challenged by the new emphasis on meeting the needs of the reader-customer, as opposed to the duty of serving the larger public. In sum, journalism's status as a profession is at the very least ambiguous, and changes in how newswork is organized, to be discussed in Chapter 4, may be further undermining the journalist's claim to status as a professional.

Objectivity in Theory and Practice

For journalists seeking recognition as professionals, the concept of objectivity extended to their activity the legitimacy of the natural sciences and satisfied a public desire for absolute norms in the face of the relativism of modernity.

As Lippmann understood the term, objectivity was a method, not a claim about the epistemological status of truth claims. As method, it meant that truth claims were to be subjected to the same continuing and rigorous scrutiny as scientific hypotheses. It is, understood this way, a critical and questioning method. Although Lippmann speaks approvingly of the scientist's "habit of disinterested realism," it seems clear that his epistemological stance is more closely aligned with the pragmatism of his contemporary, John Dewey. The truths of the scientist are working hypotheses, continuously subject to retesting, revision, and rejection.

Schudson suggests that Lippmann's forceful advocacy of objectivity played an important role in its emergence as a journalistic value. But the term, as most journalists have come to understand it, has a different significance than the meaning Lippmann attached to it. "One cannot infer from his work that daily reporters, even if they express allegiance to the ideal of objectivity, meant by it what Lippmann meant," Schudson cautions. "It is quite likely that often their concept of objectivity was simply the application of a new label to the naive empiricism which reporters of the 1890s had called 'realism.'"[21]

In this view, facts are a given in experience, and their manifest content is accessible to any competent observer. This idea has passed from vogue in philosophy and science, but it remains a widely held belief in the journalism community, which Herbert Gans has described as "the strongest remaining bastion of logical positivism in America."[22]

Objectivity may have begun as a method of systematic doubt, but in practice, in its institutionalized form, it has become a sort of naive realism. Although it appears as only one of several ethical principles in most of the codes that were promulgated beginning in the 1920s, the set of procedures that are associated with objectivity have come to be central to journalistic practice. Objectivity also became a political weapon; during the 1930s, publishers cited the need for objectivity as grounds for refusing to negotiate with the Newspaper Guild, the journalists' union, which had taken political positions.

The Rise of Social Responsibility

If the introduction of the vocabulary and methodology of objectivity can be attributed to the impact of World War I and of the propaganda and public relations industries, then the next major development in the evolution of the institutionalized discourse of journalism ethics can be attributed to the impact of World War II and the rise of the broadcast media. As the news media grew in economic and political power, there arose increasing demand for the regulation of the press. When public broadcasting was established in the 1930s, it was under much more restrictive conditions than applied to the press; radio stations were licensed and were required, as a condition of licensing, to operate in the public interest. In part, the reason for the restrictions on broadcasting was technical: although it was possible, at least in theory, for an unlimited number of newspapers and magazines to compete, the narrowness of the radio broadcast band meant that only a limited number of stations could have access to the airwaves in any community and therefore it was necessary to create mechanisms for allocating broadcast frequencies.

The idea that the press must operate independently and free of government regulation dates back to before Independence and is enshrined in the First Amendment, but the pressure for government regulation that developed in the 1940s led to an interest on the part of the press in articulating a rationale for its continued independence. It was to that end that in 1946 Henry Luce, publisher of *Time* and *Life,* created the Commission on Freedom of the Press. Luce saw the commission as an opportunity for the news industry to create mechanisms of self-regulation that might stave off more onerous government restraints. In 1947, the commission, chaired by Robert Hutchins, president of the University of Chicago, issued a landmark report titled *A Free and Responsible Press*, which made the concept of social responsibility a central theme of journalism ethics.

The Hutchins Commission was harsh in its criticisms of press performance:

> Too much of the regular output of the press consists of a miscellaneous succession of stories and images which have no relation to the typical lives of real people anywhere. The result is a meaninglessness, flatness, distortion, and the perpetuation of misunderstanding.

> The press emphasizes the exceptional rather than the representative, the
> sensational rather than the significant. The press is preoccupied with these in-
> cidents to such an extent that the citizen is not supplied with the information
> and discussion he needs to discharge his responsibilities to the community.[23]

The concept of vital information attaches to the social role of the news
media as carriers of information a moral significance: The news media
have a duty to transmit the information that we as citizens in a democracy
must have to be active participants in self-governance.

When the Hutchins Commission report was first published in 1947, it
was widely attacked by newspaper publishers, who perceived it as an attack on their editorial independence. The social responsibility theory of
the press was emphatically rejected by William Peter Hamilton of the *Wall
Street Journal:* "A newspaper is a private enterprise owing nothing whatever to the public, which grants it no franchise. It is therefore affected with
no public interest. It is emphatically the property of the owner, who is selling a manufactured product at his own risk."[24]

But the social responsibility theory, and the idea of public accountability it entails, are, at least implicitly, widely accepted within the news media.
This responsibility is the foundation of the ethical principles listed above.
What's wrong with accepting gifts from news sources, sensationalizing the
news, or giving a one-sided account of an event is precisely that such actions prevent the medium from fulfilling its social responsibility.

This theory of the role of the press makes the concept of objectivity a
central issue. In order to fulfill their obligations as citizens in a democracy,
citizens must have a reliable picture of the world and of the day's events,
that is, a picture that corresponds to the facts. Distorting that picture—
through inaccuracy, sensationalism, or bias—is direct malfeasance, while
entering into relationships that might create conflict of interest is wrong
because it may lead to distortion.

The Decline of Objectivity

Objectivity was the dominant model throughout the 1930s and 1940s, but
it came under widespread attack during and after the McCarthy era.
Writing in 1950, when McCarthy was at the height of his influence,
Richard Strout of the *Christian Science Monitor* (who later became the
New Republic's legendary "T.R.B." columnist) wrote that

The business of "straight reporting" never gives the reader much chance to catch up. If the reporter had been given the freedom of interpretive reporting customarily followed by the great dailies abroad, he could have commented as well as reported. He would have been a historian as well as a photographer with words. But he would have violated one of the dearest rules of American journalism.[25]

In the wake of the McCarthy era, objectivity began to lose its tight hold on American newsrooms, as editors gave reporters more latitude to practice interpretive reporting. And objectivity continued to come under considerable attack by opponents of the journalistic establishment in the 1960s and 1970s. With the collapse of social consensus precipitated by the Vietnam War, a critique of objective journalism emerged, along with efforts to win the admission of various styles of "new journalism," including advocacy journalism. The civil rights movement and the passing of affirmative action laws pressured the news media to employ women and minorities as journalists and to expand and improve coverage of minority and women's issues. One often heard the claim that white male journalists couldn't adequately cover the lives and interests of women and minorities, and that the addition of women and minorities would bring valuable new perspectives into the newsroom.

These ideas represented an implicit challenge to the whole ideology of objectivity, which denies the value of alternative perspectives. If everyone who follows the procedures of objective reporting and exercises sound professional judgment will produce essentially the same story, then the need for new perspectives is suspect. The viewpoints of women and minorities are, to the degree that they are new and different, seen as lacking in objectivity.

Writing in 1974, Paul Weaver described the crisis:

> The press today is an institution in limbo—an institution in that distinctive kind of trouble that comes from not having a settled idea of its role and purpose. It is in limbo because it now occupies an ambiguous middle ground between its longstanding tradition of "objective" journalism and a new movement for an "adversary journalism."[26]

Defenders of traditional notions of objectivity resisted the new forms of personal and advocacy journalism. John L. Hulteng, author of an authorized interpretation of the ASNE Statement of Principles, discusses advocacy journalism as having abandoned the search for objective reality in favor of participation in the political process. Hulteng warns that if newspapers were to abandon the goal of an unbiased news report and become organs of advocacy and opinion . . . they might well forfeit an important part of their function. They would not be as readily recognizable as an impartial proxy for the public in scrutinizing the sources of power in the society. . . . It would be a sharp retreat from the concept of responsible and undistorted journalism that has been developed in this country through the generations.[27]

The Cooke Case in Cultural and Historical Context

It was in the context of this controversy that the Janet Cooke affair took place. The Cooke case was the nexus, or flash point, of a struggle within journalism over the power to define what counts as truth, a struggle that manifested itself variously as a conflict between reporters and editors, between the "new journalism" and the old, and between a conception of professionalism wedded to a notion of objectivity and a mounting pressure for diversity—of viewpoints, of races, of genders.

Institutional politics clearly played an important part in giving the Janet Cooke case the notoriety it achieved. The focus of public attention was the fact that Cooke had lied and thereby betrayed the public trust. But debate within the journalism community tended to focus on several related issues, including the damaging impact of the Cooke affair on press credibility more generally and the right of reporters to maintain the confidentiality of their sources.

Editors tended to regard the episode as evidence that editors must have the right to exert greater control and oversight over their reporting staffs, while reporters naturally resisted this stance. "Ms. Cooke's lack of professionalism should not be used by those who would deny reporters this fundamental right," argued the national board of directors of SPJ, in a statement issued shortly after the Janet Cooke affair came to light.

For the defenders of objectivity, the case offered an historic opportunity to restore professional orthodoxy. Editors and publishers saw the case as justification for, and evidence of the need for, stronger control over the reporting process, a perspective reflected in the subtitle of the report on the case issued by the National News Council: *After "Jimmy's World": Tightening Up in Editing.*

In the foreword to the report, Norman Isaacs, former president of ASNE and one of the grand old men of American journalism, links the "Jimmy's World" scandal to larger social conflicts:

What went wrong with the American press's defenses during these past two decades is what went wrong with the whole society. As Daniel Yankelovich's new, important sociological study, *New Rules* makes clear, massive change began with the campus revolutions in the 1960s. My own ten-year span in academe taught me that the upheaval was encouraged by a vociferous minority of professors who, in my judgment, were frustrated and angry with their roles for any number of reasons. These educators instantly applauded the "do-your-own-thing" philosophy. While this self-indulgence was to sweep into all fields, it was nowhere more immediately damaging than in journalism.[28]

The impact on journalism, writes Isaacs, came in the form of the "new journalism," which Isaacs describes as

an amalgam of impressions, personal feelings, social biases and imaginative and manipulative uses of fictional techniques. It became accepted and advanced by many editors, and it stripped journalism of the one towering asset of its newsroom structure—a constant series of checks and balances under the authority of editors of character, conscience and compassion, who directed with strength and social purpose.

At least, that's one way of reading the transformations that journalism underwent in the 1960s. Another reading might treat the emergence of new styles of journalism as a challenge to the hierarchical and authoritarian structure of the newsroom, to the institution's claims to epistemic authority and, ultimately, to the very concept of professionalism, the notion that there is a specialized body of knowledge possessed by journalists that heightens their claims to knowledge and justifies the exclusion from public discourse of those who were neither professional journalists nor officially recognized experts.

The sources of this challenge can be traced, as Isaacs suggests, to the social upheavals of the 1960s. But Mercedes de Uriarte does not find their origins in a vociferous minority of frustrated professors, but rather in the anger of oppressed minorities. De Uriarte cites the criticisms of the press made by the Report of the National Advisory Commission on Civil Disorders (the Kerner Commission): "By and large, news organizations have failed to communicate to both their black and white audiences a sense of the problems America faces and the sources of potential solutions. The media report and write from the standpoint of a white man's world."[29]

The result of the riots and the Kerner report was an increasing pressure on journalism, not only to report more fully about the lives of minorities, but also to bring more minorities into journalism. This constituted a threat to the material interests of the profession—to jobs, profits, and opportunities for advancement—as well as to the philosophical rationale underlying many of their practices. One of the fundamental tenets of professionalism necessitates denial that the professional journalist reports and writes from the standpoint of a white man's world; rather, to be trained as a professional is to learn to report and write from a universal point of view. To accept that there are other equally valid points of view is to undermine one's own claim to privileged status as a professional.[30]

One consequence of this pressure was an ongoing struggle between those who believed that it was necessary to recruit and train minority journalists (Cooke is African-American) in order to adequately cover minority communities and those who regarded any such efforts as an implicit assault on the ideal of objectivity. For the opponents of affirmative action, the Janet Cooke affair presented a golden opportunity. "No attribute of Janet Cooke's received as much attention as her race in discussions of the scandal," reported David Eason, in an extensive study of the case.

> There were, for instance, no gender-based interpretations of the scandal, but there were a number of racial interpretations. These analyses focused on the merits of affirmative action programs, the pressures on minorities in organizations dominated by whites, and the effect of black-white relations within the newspaper on the reporting of black affairs.[31]

In a front page exposé of the scandal, the *Wall Street Journal* asked "To what extent do the pressures facing big-city papers to recruit and promote promising minorities cloud the initial hiring procedures as well as the decisions as to which of their stories should be published?"[32]

The pressures to integrate the newsroom and increase coverage of minority affairs were hardly the only threat to the established journalistic order. The emergence of a dissident, alternative press that challenged both the official accounts of the war in Vietnam and the acquiescent reporting of the war in mainstream media posed a similar threat. And most importantly, the unraveling of the social consensus (or at least, the illusion thereof) undermined the journalist's claim to action.

What emerged in this era were new forms of journalism that challenged the old. An increased interest in exploring, and writing about, other cultures and subcultures brought with it an increasing awareness of the relativity of one's own perspective. The work of journalist-storytellers such as Tom Wolfe and Norman Mailer spoke of worlds that could only be explored and truths that could only be revealed once one abandoned the stance of the objective reporter. What resulted was not only an undermining of the claims of traditional journalism to epistemic authority, but also its claims to moral authority.

It is a difficult thesis to prove, but this context invites an alternative interpretation of the Janet Cooke affair. The new journalism was a threat to the old, but a very difficult threat to attack head-on. If the old order was to defend its traditions and territory, a less formidable enemy would have to be discovered—or created. Cooke and her misdeeds were propelled to prominence because it served powerful interests in journalism to make an example of her case. Her transgressions became the pretext for a counter-revolution in American journalism, a reassertion of authority by an old guard whose authority had been steadily eroded for decades. What followed in the wake of Cooke's error was a reassertion of the traditional newsroom hierarchy, a banishing of the "new journalism," a "tightening up in editing," and a new fundamentalism of facts.

4

Journalism Since Cooke: The Corporate Cultural Revolution

The Increasing Irrelevance of Journalism Ethics

Journalism's conversation about ethics has not changed all that much since the 1920s, but in the past decade, journalism itself has changed dramatically. The cultural revolution currently underway in America's newsrooms is making journalism's ethical conversation increasingly irrelevant.

Granted, the conditions necessary to make ethics talk more than just talk have never been completely realized in American journalism. A French journalist who visited the United States in the 1980s commented that the wide gap between ethics talk and journalism practice led him to suspect that "ethics was being used partly as an antiseptic, partly as a public relations ploy, and partly as a means of scapegoating journalists, shifting onto their backs all the blame for the media's misdeeds."[1]

But by and large, at least in this century, the formal requirements for a meaningful conversation about ethics have been in place. In theory, at least, journalists have been professionals with a high degree of autonomy, and the newspaper has been formally pledged to a mission of service to the public. What is ethically significant about the most recent changes in the newspaper industry is that these foundations of autonomy and accountability are being systematically dismantled. The changes include:

- the introduction of new technology that reduces the level of skill required of newsworkers,

- the reorganization of the newsroom into teams, following the corporate model,
- a shift to a "market-driven" approach, in which market research replaces the expertise of the reporter as the basis for judgments of newsworthiness, and the objective of satisfying the customer replaces the goal of informing the public,
- a shift from "news" to "information," and,
- a shift in emphasis from the narrative to the visual.

Technological Innovation

Right around the time that Janet Cooke published her story, computer terminals first began to appear in American newsrooms. This new technology played a key role in reshaping the American newsroom. The most obvious impact came from the new-found ease of creating graphics on computers. Illustrations that in the past would have been difficult to produce within a newspaper's cost and time constraints were suddenly feasible for a wide range of material, and the graphics themselves looked far better, thanks to software improvements. This led to an increased emphasis on the look of the newspaper, often at the expense of the message.

Computers also made the work of editing, cutting, and pasting more efficient. The changes in technology allowed the work of typesetting and pagination, traditionally performed in the blue-collar "back shop," to be moved into the newsroom and performed by editors. Unfortunately, the switch to computers also gave rise to an epidemic of new work-related physical ailments—in the past primarily a blue-collar phenomenon—such as carpal tunnel syndrome and other repetitive stress injuries.

The reach of the new technology went beyond the emphasis on graphics or the mechanics of editorial and production procedures. Computers also provided managers with an electronic surveillance system for monitoring and measuring the performance of reporters. Once the means of quantifying job performance existed, it was inevitable that it would have a far-reaching impact on journalists. "In a job that has always been considered a "semi-professional one," writes Doug Underwood, "many newsroom employees are likely to find their jobs looking more like those of data entry workers or information processing clerks rather than the fully professional roles that they have always aspired to."[2]

Hanno Hardt, borrowing the term introduced by Harry Braverman, has labeled this trend "the de-skilling of journalists." As he points out, "The manufacture of news no longer demands professional involvement, but can be accomplished by a cheap labour force which is computer-literate and more attuned to packaging information than to exercising analytical skills."[3]

The Corporate Cultural Revolution

Accompanying the technological revolution in American newsrooms has been a cultural revolution, introduced by newspaper management. The American newsroom has traditionally had an odd status inside the larger corporation within which it operates, somewhat like the Vatican City within the larger Italian republic, allowed to operate with its own culture and values. The newsroom was insulated from the culture and the economic concerns of the larger corporation. This tradition of newsroom autonomy is a legacy of the era when most metropolitan dailies were owned by wealthy local families. Those local owners typically had a variety of incentives to maintain the autonomy of the newsroom and to forego maximizing profits: perhaps a personal stake in the future of their communities or an appreciation of the duties of civic leadership.

What is happening at many American newspapers today is a sweeping transformation of this culture. The walls that once separated the culture of the newsroom from the business culture of the surrounding corporation are being swept away. At the *Star Tribune* (Minneapolis-St. Paul), for example, the newsroom was made part of the Reader Customer Unit, to distinguish it from the Marketer Customer Unit, which services advertiser customers. The executive editor was briefly designated as head of the Reader Customer Unit, while the managing editor became the newsroom leader. Assistant city editors and assistant feature editors became team leaders, again following the corporate model. It has become customary to speak of senior editors not as editors, but as managers.

More than labels is at stake here. In one incident, the managing editor of a major midwestern daily stopped the presses to change and improve a headline deemed "too negative" for a Homes section largely supported by real estate advertising. ("Moneymaker or money pit? How do houses compare as investments? Recent history suggests that buying a home can be as perilous as riding the swings in the stock and bond markets.") In defense of this action, the managing editor cited company responsibilities as well as newsroom responsibilities and stated that the readers don't pay all of the bills.

In order to produce news more efficiently, many newsrooms have been reorganized into teams headed by a team leader—following the model of similar innovations in the corporate world—whose mission is shaped by the marketing objectives of the paper. Although the rhetoric surrounding reorganization frequently speaks of empowerment and delegating responsibility downward, the reality for many journalists is a loss of autonomy. The downsizing of middle management may mean that journalists have more latitude in deciding how goals are to be achieved, but they have less say in determining those goals.

The Public and the Reader-Customer

Newspapers have never been a place for purists. The role of the newspaper has always been to entertain as well as to inform, and the newspaper has always been a business as well as a social institution. Even at the best newspapers, the separation between the newsroom and the business office has never been complete. The autonomy and accountability of journalists has always been a sometime thing, and the conversation of journalism ethics has always been fraught with contradictions.

Nonetheless, today a new breed of corporate manager is explicitly repudiating that traditional wall of separation. "I have suggested strongly and repeatedly that the people in the [*Los Angeles Times*] newsroom need to know and understand the people in our advertising department," *Times-Mirror* Chief Executive Officer Mark Willes recently remarked. "And there has been more than one person who has pointed out the wall between the newsroom and the advertising department. And every time they point it out, I get out a bazooka and tell them if they don't take it down, I'm going to blow it up."[4]

There has long been tension between journalism's theoretical purpose and actual journalistic practices, but the cultural revolution in newsrooms means that the mission itself is being abandoned. The fundamental question of journalism ethics—How do we best realize the goal of enabling citizens to participate more fully in democratic life?—has been replaced by the market-driven question, "How do we meet what our reader and marketer-customers say are their information and entertainment needs?"

There is very little talk nowadays about readers as citizens. Rather, readers are spoken of as customers and the newspaper as a product. Increasingly, journalistic decisions are being made not on the basis of journalists' professional expertise about what it is important for the public to know, but on the basis of market research about what kinds of things customers, or potential customers, want to know.

This shift comes at a time when fundamental changes are taking place in the way that America is governed. The "end of the era of big government" has been repeatedly proclaimed. Setting aside the hyperbole, what is happening is a devolution of responsibility to more local levels of government. As responsibility for issues such as welfare and health care has shifted from federal to state and local government, the impact on citizens of decisions made at city hall and at the state legislature has increased dramatically. "This, as a result, should be a heady time for state and local newspapers," argues *New York Times* Managing Editor Gene Roberts. "But it is not. Many, perhaps most, of these newspapers are weaker in staff, news hole, and governmental coverage, than they have been in decades. A tragedy may be in the making for journalism and democracy."[5]

Roberts blames corporate management. "Often, the corporate view is hostile to governmental coverage. It has been fashionable, for some years, during meetings of editors and publishers, to deplore 'incremental' news coverage. Supposedly, it is boring, a turn-off to readers, and—what's worse—it requires news hole. Roberts acknowledges that "Government news may not be as gut-wrenching as rape, murder, airplane crashes, and other mayhem," but it is virtually the only way citizens have of keeping up with what is going on in government. "Supplying this part of the news fills a basic need of democracy."[6]

As Roberts points out, this steering of American journalism away from its public service mission

> is seldom done by corporate directive or fiat. It rarely involves killing or slanting stories. Usually it is by the appointment of a pliable editor here, a corporate graphics editor there, that results in a more uniform look and cookie-cutter approach among a chain's newspapers, or it's by the corporate research director's interpretation of reader surveys that seek simple common-denominator solutions to complex coverage problems.[7]

In selling the product, according to this new philosophy, one must find out what the customer wants and try to provide it. This new approach encourages a reorganization of the newspaper. Robert Giles, former editor of the *Detroit News*, describes how it has affected newsroom hiring:

> Adding people to the news staff, for example, will not follow the traditional formula of hiring to meet a demand for more general news coverage. . . . Editors seeking to add staff will be expected to meet a new test: how will the new staffers assist the newspaper to reach new markets of readers and advertisers it is trying to attract."[8]

The ethical implications of this stance are significant: for a market-driven newspaper, some readers are more desirable than others. Affluent readers and their communities receive better service than poor ones. Carol Bradley Shirley, an editor of the zoned *Westside* section of the *Los Angeles Times,* which serves some of the city's more affluent communities, described the real-life consequences of this economic discrimination:

> Let's say you live in Santa Monica and someone wants to put a liquor store on your block. You and some neighbors get together and make a couple of signs. You go to the city council. The *Westside* section is right there to report how you feel and to let people know about the plans for the liquor store. Others read about it and join your little group. Soon your voice grows loud and is amplified by the coverage of the *Times.* The next thing you know, the council decides that a hearing is in order. You may not get your way, but you get a hearing.
>
> If you live in South Los Angeles, as I do, you are on your own. Hundreds of people would have to show up at a council meeting before anyone in the press would take notice.[9]

The *Los Angeles Times* subsequently created a zoned section, *City Times,* to serve inner-city readers and has since abolished all of its zoned sections.

The market-driven newspaper is a response to the pressure for profitability. As newspapers have passed from independent ownership to corporate ownership, the pressures to maintain historic levels of profitability have increased. One result has been the increased use of consultants with schemes to increase efficiency of the news production process.

The *University of North Carolina Journalist* cites the example of the *Winston-Salem Journal,* now owned by Media General, where consultants introduced a system for classifying stories and the amount of work each type of story should require. "An A-1 story should be six inches or less. A reporter should use a press release and/or one or two 'cooperative sources.' He or she should take 0.9 hours to do each story and should be able to produce 40 of these in a week." The classification system, introduced in 1995, was abolished in 1996 at the urging of the new managing editor, Carl Crothers.

Gene Roberts, citing this case, pointed out the dangers of this approach:

> Classification systems put handcuffs and headlocks on reporters. They defeat the spirit of determined inquiry and thoroughness. A paper with such a system is sure to underinform its readers and become unnecessary to its community. Yet such systems are almost the logical end result of the budgetary pressure corporations are putting on their newsrooms.[10]

In an advertising campaign designed to change the newspaper's public image, the management of the *Minneapolis–St. Paul Star Tribune* announced that the goal [of the campaign] is to change Minnesotans' perception of the *Star Tribune* is [sic] a newspaper to *Star Tribune* is the brand of choice for information products. To help consumers make the change, and to illustrate the point, we need to move as far away from the newspaper as the point of reference as we can, and focus on a product that's the most different from the newspaper. . . . And work will be done to create a personality that is positive, contemporary, and appealing to our customers of information.

This shift in mission and identification has profound ethical significance. One key element of the ideology of professionalism is the idea that professionals have a duty not only to the individuals they serve, but also to the larger community. This concept of duty is also evident in the canons of medical and legal ethics; doctors are required to report communicable diseases and attorneys may not advise their clients to give false testimony because the interests of the larger community supervene.

This public dimension of journalism's professional ethics is weakened when the mission shifts from providing the information readers need as citizens to providing information that our customers value as consumers. Journalists are charged as professionals not simply to provide their readers with the information they need to have as citizens, but to give them, as Walter Lippmann put it, "the truth behind the facts," to provide them with interpretations of the day's events that are useful to them for a particular purpose—namely in their role as citizens.

The task of giving readers "the truth behind the facts" may be more problematic than Lippmann would have recognized, but it remains the central task of journalism. In our times, an essential part of this task must be to enable readers to see through the hype—to recognize media manipulation and to critically evaluate the output of the spin-doctors and the corporate and political advertising and public relations industries. Can a newspaper still have the credibility to perform that function when it is itself engaged in image management, striving to "create and maintain a personality . . . that has a positive contemporary spin that more consumers can relate to"?

Marketing the newspaper as a commodity raises other ethical issues as well. When the newspaper constructs an image of the world in which what matters is the common life, readers come to think of themselves as citizens. By contrast, positioning the newspaper as yet another consumer product adds the newspaper to the long list of products that promise satisfaction through consumption. It debases the relationship of the journalist and the reader to the message and to each other and undermines the capacity of the newspaper to serve as the carrier for the conversation through which individuals find their identity as part of a community.

In the long run, warns former *Newsday* reporter Alison Carper, the consequences of the market-driven approach are likely to be bad for both newspapers and democracy:

> The press's adoption of marketing techniques not only widens the gap between the well-informed minority and the rest of society, it has another alarming effect as well. The acceptance of these techniques represents a decisive abandonment of the social-responsibility model, the final disposal of that model's tattered remains. Without even the threads of the social responsibility model to hang onto, the press is left without a reasonable defense of the unrestrained freedom it enjoys.[11]

The Graphics Revolution

Another ethically significant transformation in American newsrooms has been the graphics revolution. Following the lead of *USA Today,* which is sold from newsboxes designed to look like televisions and which has pioneered the use of color as well as extensive use of graphics, newspapers have to a large degree transformed themselves from a narrative medium to a visual one. Any information that is really important must be carried by the picture, the headline, and the graphic treatment. As on television, stories that don't lend themselves to strong graphic treatment are likely to get poor placement in the paper. The result is a bias in favor of drama—or sometimes simply in favor of color—and against ideas.

This transformation has important implications for the newspaper's ability to serve as a forum for ideas or, for that matter, as a forum for news. On the front pages of newspaper sections, photos, illustrations, and charts typically take up about half of the available news hole. Even if it is granted that a picture may be worth a thousand words, there are differences in the kind of messages conveyed by photographs and illustrations, and the messages conveyed by text. Pictures address us at a visceral level that is more powerful than the information conveyed by text.

When Leslie Stahl of CBS crafted a news report that juxtaposed video footage of president Reagan making symbolic gestures in support of programs such as aid for the elderly with a voice-over narrative that told how his legislative policies undermined those goals, the White House responded with thanks. As White House Chief of Staff Michael Deaver later explained, the visual message so completely dominated the narrative that most viewers came away with a positive impression of the president.[12] As the visual element comes to dominate in newspapers, a similar shift in how the newspaper communicates is taking place.

The increased prominence of the visual element in newspapers has also led to changes in the news production process. In order to produce news more efficiently, the newsroom must be reorganized. Leland "Buck" Ryan, a journalism professor at the University of Kentucky, has popularized the concept of the maestro session, in which all of the players are brought together under the baton of a conductor, who synchronizes their activity for greater harmony and efficiency.

Traditionally, the graphic presentation of the news story was the final stage of the process. But that approach, which dates back to the early decades of the century, is now as old-fashioned as Henry Ford's assembly line, Ryan has argued. Modern automobile assembly has been revolutionized by the Japanese, who initiate all the elements of the process simultaneously. Ryan advocates a similar process, starting with a maestro session, where all of the elements of story production are initiated simultaneously.

Once the reporter has done some initial reporting, the assigning editor, the artist, the photographer, and the graphic designer are all brought together to plan the presentation of the complete package. At that initial meeting, decisions are made about the presentation of the package: what the headline and subheads are likely to be, the prominence to be accorded the story, and what sort of photographs and illustrations will be needed.

This approach works best when the reporter is adducing evidence or anecdotes in support of a foregone conclusion. But when the reporter starts with a hypothesis, or even just a question, then there is always the danger that as the process of investigation goes on, it will lead to conclusions very different from those decided on at the maestro session. In fact, this is what is supposed to happen in journalism: the most useful motto for journalists might well be "Things are not as they (at first) appear."

Of course, the maestro session is supposed to take place after the reporter has done some initial reporting, so it may also be that further investigation will sustain all the key elements of the initial discovery. Moreover, in theory, it is possible for the reporter to go back after further investigation and announce that her fearless quest for the truth has led to unexpected conclusions and that the page design will have to be scrapped, the headline rewritten, the photographer sent out again to take new pictures. But in an era of shrinking resources, that's a risky proposition. The danger isn't that the journalist will shrink from bringing these inconvenient discoveries to the attention of the assigning editor and oblige her colleagues to tear up their work and start over again; rather, the danger is that the maestro system creates subtle pressures on the journalist not to ask questions that may lead to inconvenient conclusions.

One consequence of this approach to reporting is that sources may increasingly refuse to talk to reporters. In a letter to a reporter from the *Los Angeles Times,* the late historian Christopher Lasch explained why he had stopped giving interviews to journalists:

> One's views appear in the form of a few isolated quotes, torn out of their supporting context and therefore misleading and incomplete, even when the reporter is well-intentioned. And when the reporter is not well-intentioned—when the story line has been predetermined in advance and the interview conducted merely with an eye to assembling supporting quotes— one's views, in the final version, often become completely unrecognizable.[13]

Another important transformation is the shift from news—information about events or issues that is important to readers as citizens and members of communities—to information that is of interest to readers as consumers and private individuals. As coverage of the day-to-day operations of government decreases, more resources are poured into coverage of health and fitness, shopping and spending, relationships, pets, and hobbies. This change isn't simply a straightforward case of giving the public what it wants— rather, it gives those readers most sought-after by advertisers what they want.

"Five or 10 years ago, your focus could be pretty much solely on content, and the question always was, 'Is this a good story?'" the managing editor of a small Virginia newspaper recently told the *New York Times.* "Now I have to think, 'Is this a story that will connect with my readers' particular lifestyles?' That's marketing, and it's something that I never had to think about before."[14]

The structure of stories is also changing. The traditional news story, in which a narrative thread is used to connect and contextualize pieces of information, is at some newspapers being replaced by a multi-layered approach, in which an abbreviated narrative is supplemented by, or sometimes simply replaced by, a set of bullets that highlights or isolates the key elements of the conclusion. There is also a tendency to run more, shorter stories. What may disappear in this process is the "why" behind the events.

What is shaping up here is a struggle for journalism's soul. The more the media address the public as consumer-customers with purely private interests, rather than as citizens who have a set of shared vital interests in public life, the more they undermine the foundation of journalism as a public practice. At some point, when content decisions are driven by ratings, or by the need to sell more papers or more ads, the resulting product can no longer be considered journalism. This progression can be seen clearly in most local commercial television news programming in the United States. The question is no longer whether their ratings-driven practices are ethical; it is whether what they do can still be called journalism. Television executives themselves now answer that question in the negative; local television news and, increasingly, national television news are entertainment, these executives concede, not a form of journalism.

Those citizens who do want information are finding ways of getting it without the intermediation of journalists; many, for example, opt to visit the home pages of candidates or countries on the World-wide Web. Advertisers, who traditionally supplied about 80 percent of the revenue for newspapers, are now finding that there are more cost-effective means of reaching potential customers: through direct mail, through specialized publications, and through the Internet. As the economic base erodes, more and more of the costs will have to be born by readers, resulting in a shrinking and increasingly elite audience.

Is Journalism Dead?

Some observers, such as Hanno Hardt, a professor at the University of Iowa, are already proclaiming the end of journalism:

> The decline of capitalism and socialism as the dominant utopias of the twentieth century is accompanied by a collapse of their respective ideological constructions of communication, participation, and democracy, including the role of the press and the function of journalists. . . .
>
> Over the course of the last century, the utopian vision of journalists as an independent, fourth estate, based on the accomplishments of journalists rather than on the institutional claims of the press, has gradually been replaced by a commercial solution, whose economic consequences have trivialized traditional, social and cultural co-determinants of journalism, including journalists, newswork, and the pursuit of public interests.[15]

Does Journalism Have a Future?

As newspapers become increasingly market-driven, the prospects for journalism dim. Civic-minded readers are a relatively small constituency, and their journalistic interests will be weighed against the interests of other market segments. From a marketing point of view, they are the audience segment that is already most loyal.

Sociologist Alan Wolfe has proposed that there are really two American middle classes: an older, more civic-minded one based in core cities and older suburbs and a new middle class that has moved to the outer suburbs,

> fleeing crime, crowding, poverty, and other dangers and irritants of the city. One of those urban irritants is politics. . . . This group generally fails to pay much attention to the civic virtues, including active involvement with issues once thought essential to the cultivation of a healthy political system. Private life is valued above political participation. Whereas the older middle class finds liberation in the public sphere and feels that an insular private life is confining, the new middle class derives happiness in private life and experiences life in the public realm as a chore.[16]

Revitalizing the public sphere may be essential to the long-term survival of newspapers and the republic. But attracting this new middle class audience in the outer suburbs seems to be the top priority for many newspaper managers, and that audience's interest in participatory democracy is limited.

It is sometimes argued that it is in the long-term self-interest of newspapers to take an active role in community-building. The decline in newspaper readership undoubtedly has multiple causes, but one probable factor is a decline in citizenship as a public value. Subscribing to a newspaper was traditionally motivated, in part, by a sense of a civic duty to be informed. If consumers no longer feel that duty, it may be at least in part because newspapers no longer address them as citizens.

Fostering a sense of citizenship may turn out to be an effective way of generating newspaper sales or increasing television audiences. Then again it may not; there may be more than a little wishful thinking behind this argument. Although the existence of journalism depends on the existence of a public that cares about public affairs, it is less clear that the future of newspapers depends on journalism. Many editors and publishers would respond that their reduced coverage of public affairs is a response to declining interest, rather than its cause. Whether newspapers can save themselves by reducing the space and resources that they devote to coverage of public affairs while increasing the space they devote to consumer information, entertainment, and the like remains to be seen.

Even if it turns out that the future of newspapers does depend on journalism—that is, that the newspaper's strongest niche in the marketplace is as a source of information and dialogue about public affairs—it is not clear that the future of the information industry depends on newspapers. Most newspapers are now subsidiaries of larger companies that see themselves as packagers and marketers of information. The existence of a vehicle that reaches a mass audience may serve the interests of democracy, but it is not necessarily the most effective way to serve advertisers and make money. If changing market conditions make the newspaper an inefficient way of serving marketer-customers, few media executives are likely to let sentimentality or an outdated ethic of public service stand in the way of progress.

Newspapers and the public that they brought into being developed concurrently with the rise of the department store and the need for a vehicle to advertise a wide range of goods to a mass market. The same dynamics of economic and technological development that led to the development of the mass-audience newspaper can be expected to contribute to its demise. The newspaper was, for a time, virtually the only way for many retailers to advertise their goods and services; today both the nature of retailing and the options for advertising have changed dramatically. The traditional department store now must compete with both mass retailers such as Wal-Mart and upscale specialty stores; and the newspaper must compete with radio, television, the community press, and direct mail.

The marketplace is also changing, as a recent report in *Business Week* details: "The middle class, which once seemed to include almost everyone, is no longer growing in terms of numbers or purchasing power. Instead, it's the top and bottom ends that are swelling."[17] As a result, many companies are adopting a "Tiffany/Wal-Mart" marketing strategy, producing different lines of merchandise to sell to high-income and low-income consumers. The newspaper, ideally suited for selling merchandise from Sears and Macy's, is not the best vehicle for reaching either Tiffany or Wal-Mart shoppers.

English communications scholar Colin Sparks has aptly summarized the cultural frame within which journalism has traditionally been practiced:

> The large circulation of the "enlightenment" newspaper is the product of the habits of a particular social group formed in what some sociologists would call "high modernity." Its readers were largely male, moderately educated, recently enfranchised, relatively privileged office workers. They genuinely believed that voting every few years was extremely important, and that they needed to be well-informed about the world in which they were significant actors. . . . Many could, as a semi-legitimate part of their working life, start the day with a coffee and glance at the paper. . . . Their domestic arrangements, very often, were of such a patriarchal character that, once home, they

could bury themselves in their paper while social reproduction went on all around them.

But, as Sparks points out, life is no longer like that:

> The highly educated, long-enfranchised and entirely cynical, but not very privileged office worker of today is more likely to be female than male. She is very skeptical about politics and public life, and places much less faith in her ability to change the world through voting. She drives to work and listens to the radio on the way. The working day legitimately starts with a cup of coffee and switching on the computer. She drives home again in the evening and of course, she has to spend her evening cleaning, cooking, washing and ironing, not to mention looking after the kids. What has disappeared from these everyday rhythms of life is the space in which the newspaper was habitually consumed.[18]

According to the most pessimistic predictions, newspapers themselves are doomed, or at least cannot survive in anything resembling their present form. Some analysts predict the collapse of classified advertising, one of the newspaper's main sources of revenue. Without substantial revenue from classified advertising, the newspaper will become much more expensive, placing it beyond the means of many current readers and reversing the democratizing trend that began in the 1840s with the arrival of the penny press. This doesn't only mean that fewer people will have access to the same information; it also means that the information that is conveyed will have to a much lesser degree the status of common knowledge that is required if the newspaper is to serve as the basis for democratic decision-making. Rather than functioning as a tool of democratic life, such a newspaper will surely serve and reflect the interests of the class of citizens able to afford it.

According to Hanno Hardt, that future is already here. The 1990s have brought the end of even the "quasi-independence of editorial work" and the adoption of a "patronage model" of the press, "which understands journalistic labor in terms of routinised technical tasks responding to specific commercial interests, such as . . . the demand of advertisers for non-controversial contextual material to help maximize the impact of commercial messages."[19] Under the new dispensation, "news will fit the requirements of a patronage system, in which journalists serve the interests of an affluent and educated commercial class consisting of businesses and their clientele as a new type of partisanship and a new understanding of public interest begin to dominate the public sphere."[20]

In this most pessimistic scenario, journalism will not survive in the commercial marketplace. Other media scholars, such as Phil Meyer, are somewhat more optimistic, though Meyer sees no guarantee that it will be newspapers that are the trusted information providers of the future. "How the information is moved—copper, wire, cable, fiberglass, microwave, a boy on a bicycle—will not be nearly as important as the reputation of the creators of that content. Earning that reputation may require the creativity and courage to try radically new techniques in the gathering, analysis and presentation of news. It might require a radically different definition of the news provider's relationship to the community, as well as to First Amendment responsibilities."[21]

Is the answer, then, to call for a return to traditional journalistic values? No. Many of those values are deeply problematic. And it can be argued that the value system that they represent, with its emphasis on objectivity and experts, as opposed to facilitating active citizenship, is partly to blame for the decline of public life.

If there is hope for journalism as a public practice and for journalism ethics as a meaningful public discourse, it must lie in a new vision of journalism ethics—one that recognizes the central importance of the public in journalism and the necessity of finding ways to reengage the public in public life.

5
Objectivity's Legacy

Is Objectivity Dead?

Objectivity may be dead, but it isn't dead enough.

Even though few journalists still defend the idea of objectivity, it remains one of the greatest obstacles to their playing a more responsible and constructive role in public life. Although the idea itself may be widely discredited, its legacy is a professional ideology that shapes journalists' daily practices.

The traditional philosophical conception of objectivity holds that "our beliefs are objectively valid when they are or would be endorsed from a perspective . . . which transcends the particularities, biases and contingencies of our own egocentric perspectives."[1] This perspective, notes philosopher Fred D'Agostino, has variously been described as the Archimedean point, "the God's-eye view," or the "view from nowhere."

Everette Dennis, former director of the Freedom Forum Center for Media Studies, wrote in 1989 that

> The upheavals of the 1960s and a reassessment of journalism's role in society, not to mention a journalistic revolution, shelved the concept [of objectivity] pretty dramatically. In time, editors and others shied away from claims of objectivity which anyone who had ever taken a psychology course knew was impossible, and opted instead for something we came to call fairness. For many, fairness was just a convenient euphemism for objectivity, but to others it represented a more thoughtful articulation of disinterested reporting that covered all the bases rather than simply "balancing" two sides.[2]

This obituary for objectivity may be premature. Objectivity is one of the central ethical principles articulated by Stephen Klaidman and Tom

Beauchamp in *The Virtuous Journalist*, one the most ambitious recent efforts to formulate a comprehensive theory of the ethics of journalism.

Ted Glasser's attack on objectivity in the May 1984 issue of *The Quill*, the monthly magazine of the Society of Professional Journalists, titled "Objectivity Precludes Responsibility," drew numerous responses, suggesting that objectivity, even if under attack, is still very widely embraced. The impact of the article was likened by one media scholar to "farting in the temple." The initial response to Glasser's essay was a spate of angry letters to the editor, but more than a decade later, the bad odor seems to have cleared and the temple still stands. Moreover, though few journalists are prepared to actively defend objectivity as an epistemological doctrine, the underlying, corresponding theory of truth remains embedded in the way concepts such as facts, distortion, and bias are used in journalism.

Objectivity rose to prominence in the 1920s at a time when journalism was facing a crisis of credibility. The simple faith in facts that had sustained a more credible generation in a less complicated era was no longer sufficient. For Walter Lippmann, this meant that journalism had to take its method from the sciences and its organizational culture from the professions. Journalism itself was to become a profession, with a claim to a specialized body of expertise and a special responsibility to the public.[3] In appealing to the scientific method and professionalism, Lippmann was borrowing from those sectors of society that had the greatest public credibility. But his attempt to ground journalists' claims to authority in appeals to science or professionalism has been, and remains, problematic.

Defining Objectivity

Journalists and media scholars talk about objectivity in at least two different senses. Sometimes, when a piece of journalism is said to be objective, what is meant is that its statements of fact, or more broadly, the pictures of reality it presents, correspond to the way things really are. But the term objectivity is sometimes also used to refer to a set of procedures that the reporter uses in order to produce those objectively true accounts. There are many journalists who practice procedural objectivity without any such epistemological commitments; for them, following the procedures of objectivity may be what sociologist Gaye Tuchman has termed a "strategic ritual," designed to fend off criticism[4]—that is, "don't blame me, I was just following procedures."

The practices of procedural objectivity have been codified by *Washington Post* reporter George Lardner Jr. as follows:

1. The reporter may relate, on his own authority, only the observable facts of an overt event—that is, what he can see and verify—immediate sense knowledge.
2. The reporter should relate what is controversial by stating the views of the parties controverting one another. This usually represents an attempt to give the "why" of an event while restricting the reporter to a narration of what is for him simply more sense knowledge, that is, what he heard the parties say about the controversy.
3. The reporter must be impartial in the gathering and the writing of both the observable facts and the opposing viewpoints. He must not let his own beliefs, principles, inclinations or even his own knowledge color the raw, overt material or the statements covering it.[5]

This definition of procedural objectivity is relatively restrictive, in that it acknowledges no place for interpretation by the reporter. Depending on which use of the term is involved, the question, "Is it objective?" can be translated as either (1) "Does it correspond to the way things are?" or (2) "Was it produced in accordance with accepted professional practices?"

Most defenders of objectivity have retreated from the claim that objective knowledge is possible in practice, taking the position that although complete objectivity can never be achieved in practice, the task of journalism is to come as close to objective truth as possible.

Facts and Pictures

Historically, the concern with objectivity has taken two different forms. The term was not widely used during the nineteenth century; concern for truthfulness in that era was focused on facts. "Facts, facts piled up to dry certitude, was what the American people then needed and wanted," muckraking journalist Ray Stannard Baker later recalled.[6] The appetite for facts may have taken root in the dramatic days of the Civil War (as Hazel Dicken-Garcia has suggested), but by the turn of the century, argues Robert Bremner, it was fueled by the social upheavals that American society was experiencing, as a generation raised on farms and in small towns came to grips with life in an environment that was "more urban, cosmopolitan and industrial than Americans had been accustomed to regard as normal."[7]

The truthfulness of newspaper reports could be established by other competent observers, but to that end it was necessary that the reports be expressed in terms that made them publicly verifiable. Grounding news reports in facts located the justification for the journalists' claim to authority in external reality itself. Facts themselves were taken to be unproblematic; their meaning was assumed to be given, available to any competent observer. Although newswriting style has changed a great deal since the 1890s, the emphasis on facts that began in that era (or earlier) is at the heart of modern procedural objectivity and is deeply embedded in the codes of professional ethics.

Just the Facts, Ma'am?

The naive faith in facts of the nineteenth century gave way in the twentieth to a recognition that the facts themselves are never enough. It became necessary to (as it has been variously put) "give the big picture," "place the facts in context," or "interpret the news." This movement has been accompanied by efforts to establish that there can be such a thing as "objective interpretation" or that, just as there can be objective facts (this is generally taken for granted), there can be an objective picture of the world.

Correspondence and Pictorial Representation

Although for many journalists achieving objectivity remains simply a matter of setting aside one's biases and digging up the facts, Lippmann recognized long ago that objectivity was much more problematic. Faith in facts was undermined by the rapid growth of the propaganda and publicity industries during and after the first World War. Facts, it quickly became clear, could be manipulated to convey the meanings that any interested party wished to attach to them. It was at this point that the problem of truthfulness began to be framed in terms of the vocabulary of objectivity and pictorial representation. What the public needed, Lippmann argued, was not merely the news—the facts—but the truth behind the facts. In the first chapter of *Public Opinion*, published in 1922, he represents this need in terms of a correspondence between the pictures inside our heads and an external reality.

What emerged in the 1920s was a recognition that the facts by themselves weren't sufficient; that it was necessary to organize and present them in a way that makes them meaningful, that forms them into "a representative picture of the world." This gave rise in the 1920s and 30s to a new breed of journalist, the political commentator (including Lippmann himself), who offered news analysis. But the latitude given to political commentators was not extended to beat reporters, and the creation of a distinct category for interpretive journalism tended to reinforce the notion that "straight reporting" is objective.

For most reporters, the rules that remained in place through the 1930s and 40s were roughly those described above by Lardner. This version of objectivity was, Donald McDonald has argued, "so narrowly defined that what was eliminated was not only opinionated editorializing in the news columns but also any opportunity for the reporter to put what he was reporting into a context which would make it meaningful." It is also, McDonald notes, a style of journalism that is easily manipulated: "When journalists confined their coverage of the late Senator Joseph McCarthy simply to what the senator said and did, far from producing objective journalism, they were producing 'the big lie.'"[8]

Many journalists were aware of this problem even at the time. Writing at the height of the McCarthy era, Douglass Cater complained that

> One of the frozen patterns that have hampered press coverage of the McCarthy charges is the distinction between the "straight" reporting of the ordinary reporters and wire-service reporters and the "interpretive" or "evaluative" reporting of the privileged few. The trouble with "straight reporting" is that it precludes investigation and asking the questions which need to be answered if the reader is to understand what is going on.[9]

Edwin Bayley, in his study of press performance during the McCarthy era, reported that debates over objectivity during the McCarthy era paralleled political divisions in the U.S. press: "All of the 'fundamentalists' on objectivity were from newspapers that supported McCarthy editorially, and all of the editors who defended interpretive reporting were from newspapers that were critical of McCarthy."[10] Writing in June of 1980, a few months before the Janet Cooke affair was to lead to a "tightening up in editing," Bayley argued that one of the legacies of the McCarthy era was a growing acceptance of interpretive reporting. But this acceptance of interpretation did not mean an abandonment of objectivity, either as an epistemological goal, or as a set of journalistic practices; rather, the concept of objective journalism was expanded to include the problematic notion of objective interpretation.

This raises an important a central question: How can the notion of an objective picture of the world be defended? When truthfulness is considered at the level of the fact, the central question becomes whether it is possible for journalists to strip away any biases that might prevent them from seeing and stating the facts clearly. In contrast, when truthfulness is considered at the level of the big picture, the question becomes one of standpoint or perspective: Is there a point of view from which we can see things as they really are?

A Simple View of Objectivity

Even today, most defenders of objectivity are not troubled by such abstract and theoretical problems as defending the concept of objective analysis or explaining the possibility of a neutral point of view. More typically, objectivity is taken to rest in the elimination of any personal prejudice and the separation of facts from values and interpretation. This simplistic understanding of objectivity clearly underlies Herbert Brucker's assertion that if objective reporting were adopted world-wide, "inevitably the ensuing world-wide access to identical facts and views would make the various nations see their common crises in all their colors, as they are, rather than through the monochrome lenses of national prejudice."[11] This view assumes that what is left when one removes one's conscious prejudices is the facts themselves; it does not acknowledge the possibility that when one sets aside one's conscious biases, unconscious biases or the biases of one's sources may remain.

It is generally acknowledged that complete objectivity cannot be sustained in practice, and yet it is defended as possible in theory and as a goal always to strive for. "None of us can ever truly be objective," acknowledges John Hulteng in *The News Media: What Makes Them Tick?*.

> Too many biases, beliefs and experiences are built into our backgrounds for us to be truly objective. Just as most of us know we can't be completely truthful, but hope to be close most of the time, so many reporters contend that it is better to aim at the objective ideal, even if you will inevitably fall short of the mark, than it is to abandon the effort and allow bias free reign.[12]

The View from Nowhere and "Objective Interpretation"

Some defenders of objectivity propose that there is a neutral or objective point of view from which the journalist can see things as they really are, and it is this impartial point of view that grounds the claim of procedural objectivity to ethical significance. Philip Meyer, author of *Ethical Journalism*, acknowledges that "it [the project of presenting reality itself] doesn't work, of course." But for Meyer the problem is a practical one, not a theoretical one: "The world is far too complex, and readers are far too impatient to wade through and analyze raw data of this sort."[13] Still, insists Meyer,

> The fact that a literal objectivity is impossible should not discourage news people from striving for it. Most of the ideals prized in our society are impossible to attain in pure form. . . . Truth is difficult to come by, verifiable fact is hard to discover and communicate, and that is exactly why we should try so hard.[14]

"The reporter," explains Meyer, "seeks to adopt a man from Mars' stance, seeing each event afresh, untainted by prior expectations, collecting observations and passing them on untouched by interpretation."[15] A similar notion underlies the oft-cited remark of Richard Salant, former president of *CBS News*: "Our reporters do not cover stories from their point of view. They are presenting them from nobody's point of view."[16]

This notion is plainly incoherent, as is the notion of observations untouched by interpretation. It is a point that the more sophisticated contemporary defenders of objectivity such as Klaidman and Beauchamp readily concede.

The Standpoint of the Reasonable Reader

Klaidman and Beauchamp, while defending the concept of objectivity, abandon the effort to ground journalistic objectivity in either "reality itself" or "a view from nowhere." Objectivity, they assert (citing the *American Heritage Dictionary*), entails "being uninfluenced by emotion or personal prejudice." Bias entails "a value-directed departure from accuracy, objectivity, and balance." They state their position in the context of a reply to a hypothetical critic:

> We would agree that there is no mirror of nature and that there are rival and incompatible sets of standards governing what will count as bias . . . and that our views rest on traditional and deeply embedded cultural perspectives about the proper role and functioning of the press.
> The difference between us and those whose views we reject is that we see nothing wrong with having a perspective; nor do we think that the fact that both journalists and consumers of news have perspectives prohibits developing standards of bias that are relevant for journalism. Of course, we assume a cultural and historical perspective. What other perspective could we reasonably take? But do journalists or the general public find fault with the stan-

dards that we contend underlie our tradition of a free and responsible press?[17]

The question is clearly rhetorical. Klaidman and Beauchamp do not believe that journalists or the general public find fault with those standards, and therein resides their (intersubjective) validity. Their benchmark for journalistic performance is what the "reasonable reader" needs to know.

> The reasonable reader is a constructed composite of reasonable news consumers, as we collectively know them. This mythical person does not do unreasonable things or have unreasonable expectations and in this respect is the personification of the community ideal of an informed person—one who has certain informational needs of the sort that quality general-news media are designed to serve. Our reasonable reader is a generalist and may be a Republican or a Democrat, a smoker or a non-smoker, a sports lover or a sports hater.[18]

Klaidman and Beauchamp argue that even though transcendent (view-from-nowhere) objectivity is impossible, standards of objectivity in journalism are not simply subjective; rather, they are intersubjectively validated. The implicit assumption captured in their discussion of the "reasonable reader" is that in all relevant respects, journalists and the general public share the same basic cultural and historical perspective. This assumption allows Klaidman and Beauchamp to relativize the notion of objectivity without acknowledging a multiplicity of communities of interpretation or addressing the ethical issues of pluralism.

Klaidman and Beauchamp use the Three Mile Island incident to illustrate the reasonable reader's information needs. In that particular case,

> the reasonable reader needs to know about the range of risk and whether there are similar nuclear plants in his or her region where a similar event might occur. As the story develops more information will be needed about how the utility and the government are handling the aftermath of the accident, new information about the accident itself and its implications, how it affects the physical and mental health of people in the area, and the implications for the nuclear power industry in general.[19]

The standard is ultimately communitarian; there is a consensus among journalists and the general public about what constitutes reasonable needs, and people who don't share it just aren't reasonable. The reasonable reader "needs to know about the range of risk and whether there are similar nuclear plants in his or her area," but apparently does not need to be informed about energy alternatives or be engaged in debates about broader issues such as the social and environmental impact of nuclear energy, the question of environmental racism (policies that concentrate hazardous waste sites in minority communities), the relevance of energy conservation, or the need for a national energy policy.

What good journalism requires, according to this viewpoint, is not a neutral standpoint, but informed judgment about what events are most important to the life of the community. But this only begs the question: "The most important aspects of contemporary life" according to whom? As a defense of objectivity, it is flawed in at least three important ways: it assumes (1) that the community the journalist serves shares a common perspective and set of interests; (2) that judgments of newsworthiness are, or at least could be, based on those public interests, and (3) that the category of facts is unproblematic. None of these assumptions holds up under scrutiny.

The reasonable reader, if we interrogate him a little further, is one who shares the values and outlook of the dominant culture. Readers who have a significantly different set of values are going to have interests that fall outside of this definition of reasonable. Thus, a reader who had an intense interest in the disposal of nuclear waste or who saw this as an important element of the Three Mile Island story, would fall outside the circle, as might, for example, any reader whose concern about institutional racism, environmental destruction, or the problem of poverty falls more than one standard deviation from the societal norm. The most important social issues that journalism must address are precisely the ones on which reasonable people disagree, and often their disagreement is not only over solutions, but also over what is reasonable and what is important. For example, ask people from different racial groups how significant the problem of racism is in American society. Whose view is the reasonable one? Is it possible that the journalist's conception of what the reasonable reader believes and wants may be one reason why newspaper readership is low in communities of color?

Journalists' own judgments of what is reasonable and what is newsworthy are inevitably more parochial than they realize. If the aspiration embodied in the concept of objectivity is to escape the parochialism of one's own point of view, the journalist cannot achieve this goal merely by imagining a reasonable reader. Rather, it can only be achieved through conversation that brings diverse perspectives into contact with each other. In the realm of philosophy, the importance of this kind of conversation has been stressed by Pragmatist philosophers such as John Dewey, who will be discussed in Chapter 7; within journalism, it has been embraced by the public or civic journalism movement, to be discussed in Chapter 8.

The concept of reasonableness turns out to import into the concept of newsworthiness the ideological biases widely shared within the culture. In *Deciding What's News* Herbert Gans has catalogued a number of these biases: ethnocentrism, altruistic democracy, responsible capitalism, small-town pastoralism, individualism, moderatism, social order, and national leadership.[20]

The Newspaper as a Picture of Daily Reality

The claim that the newspaper's role is to give a comprehensive picture of the day's events bears less and less relation to daily practice as newspapers become more market-driven. However the concept of newsworthiness may be defined within journalism, it is clear that the final product is the result of many other factors besides "evaluative judgments of relative social importance."

Klaidman and Beauchamp suggest that the organization of the news product is itself an attempt at a rational mapping of reality:

> The press often covers some types of events while excluding others for reasons that turn on evaluative judgments of relative social importance. Splitting large-city newspapers, for example, into sections such as Business, Sports, International and Style suggests a commitment to report regularly on important events in these areas. These newspapers do not generally have comparable sections on Australian News, Gambling, Scientific Research, or Professional Ethics.[21]

The suggestion here that the organizational structure of the news organization or news product is intended to reflect objective judgments about the relative social importance of various fields of human endeavor, distorts the complex play of forces that determine the allocation of space and resources.

The journalistic product emerges from a dynamic that is shaped by a number of competing forces of differing strengths and directions. Ethical considerations are only one such factor—and not the strongest. The product that emerges at deadline is the outcome of a daily struggle among these competing factors. Here, for example, is Richard Harwood:

We have great biases built into all of our newspapers in favor of certain kinds of news. . . . A bias towards the coverage of public bodies . . . a bias towards the coverage and pronouncements of politicians . . . a bias towards the coverage of the bizarre, the random event, the car crash that killed twelve people, the tornado, the murder . . . a bias towards the establishment, if you will. . . . This is a commercial function. We know that we've got to do this to hold the interest of our readers. . . . So when you ask, do we every day produce a representative picture of the world we live in, the answer is no.[22]

Economics shape the newspaper in a variety of ways. As newspapers become more market-driven, market research plays an increasingly important role in determining content. The relative balance of locally produced material versus syndicated material is partly a function of cost, as is the quantity of material included in the product. On the one hand, there are economic pressures to use the cheapest raw materials; on the other, there are union pressures, at some newspapers, to use only those local stories produced by staff reporters and editors. Advertisers also shape the product. The content of particular stories is sometimes edited to avoid giving offense to advertisers, story selection is sometimes determined by what advertisers will or will not support, and sections are created based on the demographics that they are able to attract.

The visual has always been dominant in television news, and the graphics revolution ushered in by *USA Today* has gone a long ways towards transforming newspaper from a print medium to a visual one—though the transformation may be less obvious to readers of the *New York Times* and *Wall Street Journal* than to readers of local and regional newspapers. Stories that do not lend themselves to illustration with graphs or photography do not fare well in the competition for front-page display.

The story-telling conventions of journalism also impose a certain form on the chaos. Feature stories especially are often expected to have a predictable narrative structure, with the dramatic elements of mystery, denouement, sometimes a happy ending, and frequently a moral lesson of some sort.

In addition to the unconscious ideological biases that may permeate the newsroom and the larger society, organized efforts by ideological constituencies can have a major impact on content of newspapers, not only through the direct placement of stories, but also by creating a presumption in favor of one particular point of view. The production of news is mediated through such institutions as the press conference, the spokesman, the press kit, and the public relations office. This shapes cov-

erage in favor of the elements in society that are powerful enough and organized enough to generate press materials, hold press conferences, and
otherwise garner media attention.

The prominence accorded to any given story is also a function of mix
(what other stories are going to appear on the page on a given day) and
news hole (how much space/time is available, and whether it is a busy or
slow news day).

It might be argued that all of this analysis merely shows what many defenders of objectivity readily concede—that objectivity is impossible to
achieve in practice. They do not concede that it is incoherent as an ideal.
On this view, journalists could, in theory, "carve up the world at the joints"
and present a picture of the world that corresponds to the most important
features of daily reality. As a practical matter, such a hypothetical reorganization is "possible" only in the most abstract sense of the term; the competing ideological, economic, and other vectors that shape the news product are deeply entrenched in social reality. Moreover, the very question of
how to parse up the world into more "objective" beats—even if we translate this into relativistic terms such as "most relevant to compelling human interests"—does not lend itself to any simple or objective solution.
The questions of which aspects of reality are the most important or newsworthy are highly contested.

Setting such considerations aside, the claim that there could be a more
objective organization of news beats, and hence a more objective picture
of the world, is a case of seduction by metaphor. Both "observe" and
"world" are problematic. To describe journalists as "observing" puts a rep-
resentationalist spin on what journalists actually do. What journalists do,
for the most part, is to follow a beat whose routines and agenda are shaped
by the (usually bureaucratic) news sources around whom the beat is structured. They do not so much observe as listen or transcribe. Their subject is
not "the world," but the news sources who are authorized to offer interpretations of it.

Lippmann's version of objectivity was sophisticated enough to acknowledge that the subject of objective journalism was not the elusive "reality itself," or something that is perceived from "a view from nowhere," but
rather what is given to us in the accounts of experts—experts whom
Lippmann envisioned as dispassionate social scientists. Whether objectivity is any more accessible to social "scientists" than it is to journalists is
doubtful; the fractiousness of ideological disagreements in the social sciences suggests that it is not.

What does deserve further examination is the nature and function of the "experts" whom journalists rely on to supply interpretation of the news. These experts rarely qualify as dispassionate social scientists. The conventions of objective journalism have given rise to an entire industry of think tanks and policy institutes whose function is to give representatives of entrenched political or economic interests the credentials they need to serve as authorized "knowers." Having such credentials gives these "experts" access to the media, which in turn legitimates both their status as experts and the status of their institutions. Tracing the rise of these institutions in the 1970s and 80s, Edward Herman and Noam Chomsky observe that

> Many hundreds of intellectuals were brought to these institutions, where their work was funded and their outputs were disseminated to the media by a sophisticated propaganda effort. The corporate funding and clear ideological purpose in the overall effort had no discernible effect on the credibility of the intellectuals so mobilized; on the contrary, the funding and pushing of their ideas catapulted them into the press.[23]

Lawrence Soley, in an extensive study of the role of "news shapers" argues that "reporters become convinced of the expertise of news shapers merely because other journalists have quoted them."[24] Herman, Chomsky, and Soley share the view that journalists' reliance on experts infuses the news with a heavy bias in favor of the most powerful sectors of society—that is, government and corporate interests. Part of Soley's proposed solution is to broaden the range of sources that journalists call on to interpret the news. That would undoubtedly make reporting more balanced, but it is not clear in what sense such reporting would be more objective. Rather, Soley's proposal seems to recognize that responsible journalism can neither be a-perspectival nor have the perspective of the "reasonable reader," but should be multi-perspectival.

The Problematic Nature of Facts

The emphasis on facts in journalism is grounded, at least in part, in a desire to model journalism on science. The plausibility of the claim that the set of journalistic practices that constitute procedural objectivity is capable of yielding objective knowledge about the world is based on two fundamental premises: (1) that journalists' methods of gathering information are essentially similar to scientific methods of observation, and (2) that scientific observation yields objective knowledge. This second claim is widely challenged even within the scientific community. As for the first claim, it is easily demonstrated that the actual practices of journalistic information-gathering are very different from the model of scientific observation upon which the premise is based.

Underlying the edifice of journalistic objectivity is an unquestioned faith in facts. *Washington Post* reporter Lou Cannon observes that "Objective reporters accept on faith the importance of the observed event—of something that can be seen, heard, smelled or felt. They believe, in Brucker's term, that there are 'agreed facts' of such an event from which the truth can be derived. Objective reporting does not admit that the selection of facts, even by trained reporters, is a subjective process."[25]

Cannon rejects the possibility of objectivity, because the selection of facts is a subjective process, but he does not reject the "givenness" of the facts themselves. This is precisely what sociologists such as Mark Fishman have challenged: "the assumption contained in the concept of news selectivity that all events (both the reported and the unreported) are objective, unformulated entities 'out there' in the newsworld, and that they are 'given' in perception and available to any competent, clearheaded observer."[26]

News events are not given, but are rather the product of newswork, argue Fishman and Tuchman. "It makes no sense to speak of pure, unformulated events. Any event arises in the relationship between a knower (employing schemes of interpretation and schemes of relevance) and behaviors in a material world (which are in and of themselves either meaningless or unknowable)."[27] Or in Tuchman's words, "the act of making news is the act of constructing reality itself, rather than a picture of reality. . . . Newswork transforms occurrences into news events."[28]

The plausibility of the claim that journalists observe and record "raw data" (Philip Meyer's term) may trade on an image of journalists observing natural phenomena such as earthquakes and fires or overt human actions such as shootings. But this sort of first-person observation by journalists forms the basis for only a small part of news production. Far more of what journalists report is "cooked data"—staged events such as press conferences, information released by official sources, records of commercial transactions, or events that have been created for the sake of their symbolic significance.

Facts as Social Constructions

If journalistic facts aren't a given in the nature of reality, what are they? They are shared interpretations of reality produced by the interaction of newsworkers and (to use Mark Fishman's term) authorized knowers. Authorized knowers, such as the desk sergeant at the precinct station or the researcher at the Centers for Disease Control, derive their authority from their position in a structure that produces knowledge. Labeling facts as interpretations is a way to emphasize that they express one possible construction of events and that there always exists the possibility of other interpretations from other points of view. Facts are thus to be understood as (in Alvin Gouldner's term) decontextualized discourse.

The missing context in a factual proposition is the part that identifies the point of view (subjectivity) from which the object appears as it does; the assertion of facticity locates the truth of the proposition in the object itself. Some interpretations may be so widely shared that they cannot usefully be identified with any particular class or interests, but, in the more interesting cases, a consequence of objective discourse is precisely to "privilege"—that is, to place beyond the boundaries of debate—a particular interpretation of reality, that may well be in conflict with other interpretations. When there is no conflict over interpretation or when conflict is resolved through an open process that results in consensus, this privileging of information is unobjectionable. But more often, privileging simply forecloses the possibility of open debate.

Those uses of objectivity that privilege one interpretation of reality in preference to other interpretations in the social and political arena may be labeled as ideological. Virtually everyone shares an interpretation of reality in which France exists; thus propositions about France are not, in and of themselves, ideological. Propositions about the Malvinas (the Argentine name for what the British call the Falkland Islands), alcoholism, or terrorists are, however, more problematical.

The widely reported "facts" about alcoholism may be taken as a case in point. It is now very widely accepted within our society that alcoholism is a disease. However, few realize that this interpretation is of very recent origin. Previously, people who are now diagnosed as alcoholics and channeled into medical and psychological treatment were labeled as habitual drunkards, and their actions were interpreted within the framework of a more moralistic conceptual scheme. The transformation was not the result of any scientific breakthrough that revealed an organic cause for the disease; no such cause has ever been found. Rather, we seem to be experiencing a paradigm shift (a process that is still taking place) in which one vocabulary has been adopted and another abandoned.

That transformation parallels the emergence of a social formation—a medical/psychological bureaucracy—that appropriated social jurisdiction over the handling of problem drinkers. This bureaucracy imposed a vocabulary upon problem drinkers and their behavior that interpreted their conduct in terms reflecting a medicalized worldview, while also legitimizing its own claim to jurisdiction. Alcoholism, a term unknown during most of the nineteenth century, is now accepted as social fact, an element of social reality to which the public has reacted by building treatment centers and passing legislation. Alcoholism has become a key category in terms of which individuals form their self-concept.[29]

The introduction of the discourse of alcoholism into the body of public knowledge is a small but telling example of the role that changes in language play in altering the ethical norms of a society, as well as the role that the news media can play in moral change. The adoption of the vocabulary of alcoholism transformed public perception of the problem drinker from an object of moral condemnation to an object of the same sympathy usually extended to victims of traditionally recognized diseases. At the same time, this new vocabulary promotes a mechanistic and deterministic conception of human agency, replacing a conception that emphasized individuals as agents morally accountable for their actions. Thus, the facts about alcoholism can be seen as facts only relative to a scheme of interpretation, which must be understood as a human construction shaped by human interests.

What's Wrong with Objectivity in Practice?

It might still be argued that even if the practices of objective journalism do not produce objective knowledge, their impact is beneficial or at least benign. But a strong case can be made for the view that these practices are in fact harmful, in several ways.

Objective reporting can be irresponsible. The practices of journalistic objectivity severely restrict the accountability of the reporter for the truthfulness of the information he or she transmits, provided that the information is provided by an authorized knower. In practice, the latitude that journalists have to seek and present diverging opinions or contradictory evidence varies, but within strict interpretations of objectivity it is usually very limited. Howard Kurtz, in explaining why the press failed to alert the public to the impending scandals that took place at the Department of Housing and Urban Development in the 1980s, places the blame squarely on objectivity: "Trapped by the conventions of objectivity, most newspapers would simply quote both sides—Pierce Says Housing Shortage

Nonexistent, Critics Disagree—even though one version was demonstrably false."[30]

By focusing on facts and overt events, objective reporting devalues ideas and fragments experience, thus making complex social phenomena more difficult to understand. It is arguable that the relative incoherence of public discourse over such important social issues as the economy or the health care system is attributable in large part to this emphasis on events and facts, which decontextualizes relevant information.

Even journalists who no longer believe that the pictures they are creating correspond to some absolute reality continue to define their role in terms of creating pictures—that is, generating accounts of "news." This focus privileges accounts of events—even trivial events or "pseudo-events" staged for the sole purpose of being recorded by journalists, at the expense of many other kinds of information that journalists could generate. Relatively little space in newspapers is devoted to how-to journalism or to journalism that creates a forum for dialogue between conflicting interests or points of view.

6

The Myth of Neutrality and the Ideology of Information

The Myth of Neutrality

Another obstacle to more constructive and responsible journalism, closely related to the myth of objectivity, is the myth of neutrality. The journalists' claim that "we don't make the news, we only report it" functions implicitly—and frequently explicitly—as a denial of responsibility: Don't blame us, we're just the messengers, and as messengers, we are only doing our duty. It also functions as an injunction: Journalists must resist the temptation to step outside the role of neutral observer and messenger; even when their motives are altruistic, they risk undermining both their own objectivity (that is, their ability to see things impartially) and their credibility.

Robert Haiman, former executive director of the Poynter Institute for Media Studies, expresses this injunction in theatrical terms: journalists must remember that their place is in the audience, never on the stage. The messenger metaphor carries with it strong ethical implications: Messengers are servants, and paramount among their duties are faithfulness and truthfulness. Their job is, in the most restricted sense, to carry messages, and they must not alter the message to suit their own interests, must not dally in delivering the message, and must not accept other employment that would interfere with their duties to their master. These duties translate to the ethical principles regarding objectivity, fairness, accuracy, sensationalism, conflict of interest, and so on.

Of course, the news media do not cause earthquakes, volcanic eruptions or lopsided defeats for the home team, and "don't blame us" is a perfectly reasonable response to those who turn their distress over these events into anger at the messenger. All too often this defense is used for a broader and more questionable purpose—to disavow responsibility for how the news is reported.

There are three different premises that contribute to the exculpatory force of the assertion that journalists do not make the news: an implied distinction between speech and action, an implied distinction between the "real world" and the mirror world of journalism, and an implicit claim that the journalist could not have done otherwise:

1. *Speech Versus Action.* The exculpatory force of the claim that "we didn't do it, we merely reported it" rests at least in part on a distinction between speech and action and on an implicit claim that under ordinary circumstances only action is morally significant. Journalists are accountable for the truthfulness of their reporting, but not for its consequences (except, presumably, in cases such as shouting "fire" in a crowded theater). This response is one that journalists frequently offer when criticized for reporting too much "bad news."

2. *The Real World Versus the Mirror World.* Haiman's stage metaphor represents journalism as something that happens off-stage, outside of the world that journalists are supposed to represent. The plausibility of this metaphor seems to rest upon a model of journalism in which the reporters/observers and the observed exist in separate domains, with reporters observing their subjects as if through a one-way mirror, a situation in which observation and reporting indeed have no impact on the events observed.

By locating the journalist off-stage, the myth of neutrality obscures the increasingly powerful role of the news media in society. The role that the news media play in shaping not only political discourse but also political institutions, in defining public agendas, and in setting the terms of moral discourse are rendered invisible.

3. *No Choice.* Journalists do not exactly claim that they are "only following orders," but part of the concept of journalistic objectivity is that there are objective criteria that determine newsworthiness, and when an event has been determined to be newsworthy, the journalist has no choice but to publish. Reality itself dictates the journalist's actions.

Whereas the first two exculpatory premises in effect deny that the journalist really does anything, the "no choice" argument acknowledges that reporting often does have morally significant consequences. To justify the conduct of journalists that may result in harm to others, journalism's institutionalized discourse has produced a variety of arguments acknowledging that reporting does have morally significant consequences, but maintaining that the reporter must proceed without regard to consequences and "let the chips fall where they may."

The arguments in support of this position are sometimes Kantian in their emphasis on principle (A reporter's first duty is to the truth.) and sometimes consequentialist (In the long run, it is in the best interests of the society as a whole.). A great deal of ethical discourse in journalism focuses on the question of whether there are instances in which this prima facie duty to tell the truth may be overridden by a concern for consequences. Some cases involve issues of national security, while others involve issues of privacy or compassion. Also implicit in the assertion that "we don't make the news" is the counterfactual conditional: If journalists did make the news, as opposed to merely reporting it, they would bear a greater responsibility for what they report.

The problem with this conception of the journalist's role is that it fails to acknowledge both the active role that journalists play in making the news and the increasingly central role that the news media play as social institutions.

Journalists as Newsmakers

The notion of objective reporting relies heavily on the image of the reporter as observer, exposing him- or herself to the flow of experience and then culling from the totality of experience the most significant events. But the actual practice of newsgathering is quite different. Very little of what is counted as news consists of actual first-hand accounts of the natural world. Most reporting consists of second- or third-hand accounts of what someone said happened, is happening, or is otherwise important. And the accounts reporters rely on cannot simply come from any source; generally, to be acknowledged as facts, they must be taken from sources recognized as authorized knowers—that is, experts or authorized representatives of authority. Most of the facts that reporters deal with are bureaucratic facts, interpretations of reality assembled and disseminated by bureaucracies, reflecting their priorities and their perspectives. A reporter's beat preselects which elements of the day's experience the reporter is to take as newsworthy; in practice, the beat is a list of persons whom the reporter may treat as reliable sources of news.

Fishman's observation of the daily routine of a California newspaper reporter assigned to the justice beat supports this claim:

On any beat, there are an infinite number of activities to which the reporter could potentially be exposed. . . . The [justice reporter's] territory conceivably encompassed . . . several thousand square miles containing 500,000 potential law-breakers . . . three law enforcement agencies . . . four penal institutions . . . two juvenile facilities . . . two entire court systems . . . an extensive drug subculture . . . a moderate size skid row area . . . and so on.

. . . Out of the potentially infinite (and indefinite) expanse of his beat territory, [the justice reporter's] round narrowed his coverage to three official agencies of social control: the city police, the county sheriffs, and the superior court. . . . The reporter's round simply excluded him from all juvenile facilities and adult penal institutions, the FBI branch office, two municipal police departments in the Purissima region, the local chapters of the American Civil Liberties Union, National Lawyers Guild, and American Bar Association, a community legal collective, and all private security and detective agencies. But more important than this, the justice round steered the reporter away from all institutions (or "communities of action") relevant to criminality and law enforcement which were not formally constituted or bureaucratically organized. Specifically, the journalist had no regular contact with the underlife of prison and jails; the unofficially sanctioned practices of law enforcement, judicial and penal personnel; the entire spectrum of deviant subcultures (from the world of winos to the stable corporate arrangements for price fixing); and the local markets for stolen goods, illegal drugs and pornography.[1]

The reporter could, of course, expand his range of sources to include people with other perspectives, for example, victims or defendants. But this is problematic for several reasons. As a practical matter, it would be much more difficult and time-consuming than collecting information from fewer official sources, and the autonomy that journalists have to draw on unofficial sources varies greatly. It would also be difficult to claim that such an approach would be "more objective"; rather, it embodies a tacit acknowledgment that responsible journalism must be multi-perspectival.

In daily operations, then, the reporter is dependent on a network of (to use Mark Fishman's term) authorized knowers. The reporter's ability to write news stories based on this bureaucratically supplied information depends on being able to accept the truthfulness of that information as a given. These authorized knowers are also not simply the objective observers of reality that the theory of objectivity presupposes; they are its producers.

Also concealed by the doctrine of neutrality is the reflexivity of the newsmaking process, the inevitably interactive relationship between reporter and source. The presence of the reporter (and especially, the presence of the camera) transforms the event from private to public. The news media did not just report the news of the two whales trapped in Arctic ice or of two-year-old Jessica trapped in an abandoned well. Rather, they transformed those obscure occurrences into news, invested them with symbolic meaning, and by their activity shaped their outcomes—the sending of icebreakers, the outpouring of donations. These may not be typical news events, but what is typical is the transformative impact of news coverage. When the newspaper reports that interest rates will rise next Tuesday, it doesn't merely report a fact; it also alters what will happen as a consequence.

Fishman's prime example of the manufactured nature of news events is the crime wave he observed in New York City in 1976. During the course of this supposed wave of crimes against the elderly, which occupied the attention of the city's media and public, Fishman discovered statistical evidence that the number of crimes against the elderly had actually declined compared with a year earlier. As he observed, "Something in the news production process was creating the news. What was it?"[2] Fishman ultimately traced the beginning of the crime wave to a series of stories about the elderly written by a reporter for the *New York Daily News,* with information provided by the newly created Senior Citizen Robbery Unit (SCRU) of the city's police department.

> The police unit let him know they felt beleaguered, understaffed, and that they were fighting a battle that deserved more attention. After he finished the feature stories, the reporter was able to follow up the series with several reports of specific incidents because SCRU officers were calling him whenever they knew of the mugging or murder of an elderly person.[3]

Soon, the city's other media increased their coverage of crimes against the elderly. Individual crimes that would have gone unreported before were now connected by a common theme. As coverage escalated, politicians seized hold of the issue. The mayor grabbed headlines by declaring a war on crime, expanding the SCRU, and increasing the priority of crimes against the elderly within the police department. "Thus, a week and a half after the coverage started, the police wire was steadily supplying the press with fresh incidents almost every day. And when there was an occasional lack of crimes, there was plenty of activity among police, politicians and community leaders to cover."[4]

The ideal of objectivity means that the journalist makes every effort to record reality just the way it is, but that becomes impossible when reality interacts with the journalist. Defenders of traditional ethical norms address these interactions in terms of manipulation. Daniel Boorstin coined the term pseudo-event to draw a line between the unreflexive reality that it is the journalist's task to record and a false, manipulated reality, created for the journalist's benefit. A pseudo-event

> is not spontaneous, but comes about because someone has planned, planted, or incited it. Typically, it is not a train wreck or an earthquake, but an interview. It is planted primarily, (not always exclusively) for the immediate purpose of being reported or reproduced. . . . Its occurrence is arranged for the convenience [of the journalist]. Its success is measured by how widely it is reported.[5]

William Rivers, Wilbur Schramm, and Clifford Christians echo Boorstin's distinction between reality and pseudo-events: "For a journalist to be more than ordinarily suspicious these days is a step towards reporting the news behind the facade."[6]

The claims underlying this concept of the pseudo-event are that there is a real world beyond the world of pseudo-events and that although the journalist may be occasionally permitted to indulge the really imaginative publicity stunt, he or she is obliged to separate news from publicity and to make certain that readers or viewers can make the same distinction. But the distinction seems to have lost its usefulness.

Real events, Boorstin suggests, are things like train wrecks or earthquakes. If that is the case, then the vast majority of what is covered in the news media must be counted as pseudo-events—images of reality constructed not only by the intentions of the subject, but also by the conventions and technologies of the news media themselves. When President Bush chose to give a speech in a flag factory or when President Clinton flew to Yellowstone to deliver an environmental message, the event was shaped for, and by, the presence of the camera. The reality portrayed by television becomes more real than "real" life, because it is public—in a sense in which few actions of private individuals can be—in a mass-mediated era. Journalism scholar John Pauly argues that

> In a familiar sense, the media call society into existence by creating the infrastructure of everyday life, connecting and coordinating society's parts and investing those connections with meaning. But "the media" are themselves symbols with which Americans habitually think about modernity. The media create a stage upon which modern society plays itself out, but they soon become characters in that drama as well.[7]

This role of the news media in constructing our image of reality came under public scrutiny during the 1996 Summer Olympic Games, when NBC tailored its coverage to achieve higher ratings among a targeted audience—women—by emphasizing gymnastics and human interest profiles of the participants, while virtually ignoring such traditional staples as boxing. Although NBC came under considerable criticism for this strategy and for virtually ignoring foreign competitors, one would be hard-pressed to say what an "objective" presentation of the games would have looked like. The Olympic Games were closely followed by the Republican and Democratic national conventions, which had been transformed by their organizers into tightly scripted television programs, designed for television consumption. Do those events now qualify, under Boorstin's definition, as "pseudo-events?" If so, it would be difficult to find events in American political life that do not fall under that heading.

Some, like Walter Karp and J. Herbert Altschull, have claimed that it is erroneous to ascribe power to the news media. They argue that power resides elsewhere (in the hands of an elite or, in the case of political reporting, in the hands of the Congress) and that the media are merely instruments or agents of power. But it seems better to say that the news media are a battleground where struggles over meaning and for power are waged. Although it is indisputable that those who have the most power in this society also exert the greatest control over (and through) the mass media, it is also true that the mass media have institutional interests and values that cannot be simplistically identified with the interests of any particular group.

Rejecting the observer model goes beyond arguing that journalists make the news, that the reports in the newspaper are more properly read as inventions—or at least as interpretations—than as pictures or discoveries. A more complete concept of the news media as actors in society involves recognizing and giving an account of the ways in which the emergence of the news media has transformed social practice. The often-lamented transformation of public discourse that has resulted in "sound-bite politics" is only one example. On the campaign trail, the audience remains, but as a prop; the politician's discourse no longer takes the dialogical form dictated by face-to-face encounters; rather, the politician now speaks the language of the media, in images.[8]

The result is what has been termed "hyper-reality" by Umberto Eco, Jean Baudrillard, and others. As the mass-mediated reality comes to supersede a social reality based on face-to-face encounters, the traditional ground of journalistic practice is eroded. Leaders, in a traditional sense of the term, emerge from social institutions within a community, but what characterizes much of contemporary life is precisely the collapse of these institutions. Community organizations, in this context, are more typically small and struggling efforts to create an organized community than evidence of the existence of one. So when the reporter searches for leaders to speak authoritatively for or about the community, she or he is actually engaged in the process of conferring legitimacy and creating leadership.

The News Media as More Than Information Services

The emphasis on information is explicit in all of the media's major codes of professional ethics. The ASNE Statement of Principles contains this assertion: "The primary purpose of gathering and distributing the news is to serve the general welfare by informing the people and enabling them to make judgments on the issues of the day."[9] The SPJ Code of Ethics holds that: "Members of the Society of Professional Journalists believe that public enlightenment is the forerunner of justice and the foundation of democracy. The duty of the journalist is to further those ends by seeking truth and providing a fair and comprehensive account of events and issues."[10]

Journalism's ethics focus so intensely on the role of the news media in the transmission of information that other very important—and ethically significant—social roles played by the news media are completely overlooked. There are at least three critical roles the news media play in the life of their communities that go beyond merely providing information: they construct a common reality, they bring a public into being, and they are an important vehicle by which the moral values of the community are circulated. The news media play a central role in constructing the picture of the world that people who live in complex modern societies carry around inside their heads. That picture may vary in its details from head to head, but having a shared body of information is what gives us a common culture.

The News Media and the Construction of Social Reality

It has become commonplace to say that facts are social constructions and that journalistic facts are constructed by journalists, but that doesn't explain the social significance of this activity. Traditionally, the journalist has been characterized as observer, gatekeeper, or messenger. Each of these metaphors suggests different aspects of the media role, but they all suggest that the news media are essentially servants of the public. The observer merely records events, but does not cause or participate in them. The gate-keeper screens out unreliable messages, ones that might distort the master's perception of reality. The messenger operates at the periphery of our kingdom; like a periscope, telescope, or microscope, the messenger extends the reach of our senses, fills in gaps in a map that is primarily grounded in our own unmediated experience.

The servant model is consistent with the widely held "limited effects" theory, which maintains that the news media have a very limited ability to influence people and events. The messenger model may have offered a plausible account of the role of the news media throughout the periods of human history in which face-to-face interaction was primary and mediated information was secondary or peripheral. Before the introduction of printing, virtually all human communication was face to face. But in the last two centuries, the news media and, more broadly, the mass media have come to play an increasingly central role in shaping social reality. We act in the world on the basis of the pictures (and meanings, stereotypes, and symbols) inside our heads. These images and meanings are a synthesis of our own direct experience and mediated experiences of events that occur in another place and time and are communicated to us by other individuals or through the mass media. In the modern era, the news and mass media have come to play a rapidly increasing role in shaping the contents of the pictures in our heads. Within the mass media, over the last 40 years television has risen to a position of clear dominance. "TV provides the dominant system of spiritual, political, moral and social values by which we live," insists Elayne Rapping.[11]

The media are an arena for a fundamental struggle in our culture over the power to decide whose knowledge claims are to be taken as authoritative, to define the rules and limits of rational discourse, and to determine who is to be included or excluded as a legitimate participant in public discourse.

This power, and the struggle over it, is a central dynamic of social life, as Michel Foucault has pointed out:

> In a society such as ours, but basically in any society, there are manifold relations of power which permeate, characterize and constitute the social body, and these relations of power cannot themselves be established, consolidated nor implemented without the production, accumulation, circulation and functioning of a discourse. There can be no possible exercise of power without a certain economy of discourses of truth which operates through and on the basis of this association.[12]

When Foucault speaks of an "economy of discourses of truth," he means an ensemble of apparatuses much broader than just the mass media, but it seems clear that the mass media, and more specifically the news media, play a central role in the production, circulation, and functioning of the discourses that sustain the social order.

That role has become more powerful as the news media have supplanted the church and the marketplace as the prime disseminators of information. Just as public discourse sustains the relations of power within a society, the relations of power within a society determine the direction and boundaries of public discourse. To the degree to which any social entity is able to command the attention of the media (and dictate the terms of coverage), it is able to define the representation of reality in ways that reflect its interests. Thus, the ability of the Pentagon, White House, and other official entities to dictate the terms of how the Gulf War was represented in the news media influenced public perceptions of the war that reinforced the credibility and public approval of those institutions.

Recently, critics and scholars of the news media have rejected the conventional information model, offering theories that assign the news media a more pervasive and constructive role. James Carey, for example, distinguishes between the transmission function, which is emphasized in codes of ethics, and the ritual function of communications, which is almost entirely ignored:

> A ritual view of communication is directed not toward the extension of messages in space, but toward the maintenance of society in time; not the act of imparting information but the representation of shared beliefs.
>
> If the archetypal case of communication under a transmission view is the extension of messages across geography for the purposes of control, the archetypal case under a ritual view is the sacred ceremony that draws persons together in fellowship and commonality.[13]

Elayne Rapping, in *The Looking Glass World of Nonfiction Television*, stresses a related point: The structure and content of local television newscasts are designed not so much to create an understanding of local or world events as to create a sense of community and belonging.

The news media also play a key role in constructing what sociologists call the "social imaginary": To think of oneself as a citizen is an act of the imagination. We all live in what Benedict Anderson has termed "imagined communities,"[14] and it is participation in a shared discourse circulated by the media that makes us members of those communities. The American revolution became possible, in part, because the newspapers of the era spread the idea to its readers that they were not merely Virginians, or New Yorkers, or royal subjects, but Americans. Journalism is only possible in a world in which readers imagine themselves as citizens. Whether readers have this concept of themselves depends on the nature of the discourse that surrounds them. When a newspaper addresses its readers as citizens, it addresses them as parts of a "we" that shares common concerns and mutual obligations.

The Creation of a Public

Alvin Gouldner argues that it is the sharing of a common base of information among strangers that constitutes this collection of strangers as a public; newspapers thus have played an instrumental role in bringing publics into being. As Gouldner argues, "News . . . has a cosmopolitanizing influence, allowing persons to escape provincializing assumptions, and thereby enabling them to *compare* their conditions with others. News allows alternatives to be defined as 'realistic,' by showing different conditions to exist already."15 Gouldner argues that this function of the news media enhances public rationality, but it must also be seen as inherently destabilizing to the social order. The news media break down the walls that segregate different moral communities. This breakdown occurs not only through the "cosmopolitanizing" influence created by the importing of information about other ways of life, but also by the transformation of large areas of social life from private to public. The domain of topics considered too private to discuss— especially those related to sexuality—has shrunk to the vanishing point because the media do talk about them. Practices within the family or within the community come under public observation (actual or potential), and the moral discourse of the community is carried into the walls of the home.

The Moral Function

The news media play a dynamic role in shaping the morality of the society they serve. All ethical discourse is based on a sense of *we*: that you and I are part of some larger community and that the consequences of being part of that *we* need to be worked out. That sense of being part of *we*— and our understanding of the scope of that belonging—emerge from the totality of the communities and conversations or discourses in which we participate. The news media are not the only way that this discourse is circulated, but they are a very important one. We live in an era in which mass communications predominate, providing the context within which inter-personal communications take place and are understood.

It seems likely that the moralistic tone of early nineteenth-century news reporting both reflected and fostered similar thought and speech among its readers. It is also likely that the banishment of explicit moral judgments from the news columns, which came with the introduction of the objec-tive style of reporting, has had, for better or for worse (or perhaps both), an equally significant impact on current public discourse. When Alasdair MacIntyre tries to explain the incoherence of much of today's moral dis-course, he overlooks one important possible explanation: What we know of this vocabulary we know largely through the mass media, which present it only in fragmentary and limited ways.

When societal values change, the engine of that change is language, and the mass media are the medium for the circulation of that language. Even—perhaps especially—without explicit moral language, new vocabulary en-courages us to see the world in new ways. The term "sexual assault" helped to shift the perception of rape from an act of passion to a crime of violence. When the word "ecology" came into widespread circulation, it reframed public perception of the natural environment as a living and interdependent system of which we are a part and to which we have some obligations.

This moral function of the news media is arguably their most important function. The news media are one of the most influential means for circu-lating the moral norms of the society, for circulating the conversation in which disagreements about those norms are debated and resolved, and for circulating the new vocabulary that signals changes in those values. For example, the introduction of words such as "sexism" and "homophobia" signaled changing social attitudes while also making problematic some forms of conduct that had been taken for granted before.

Thus, there are profound ethical implications when a newspaper shifts from seeing itself as being fundamentally in service to its community to being in service to its customers, and when it shifts from addressing its readers as citizens to addressing them as consumers. To the degree that it ceases to place its duty to the community first and to address its audience as members of a community, the newspaper is abandoning both journal-ism and its larger moral role.

The Impact of the News Media on Social Structure

"Culture is the means by which we pass on to new generations our values, beliefs and hard-won wisdom," notes Elayne Rapping. "But, as the term 'mass communication' implies, the rise of home TV has taken this crucial socializing function out of our hands and transferred it to commercial network executives."[16]

What image of social reality do the news media create and transmit? We can begin with one broad generalization: Journalism produces images through which bureaucratic institutions define and dominate social reality. There are conflicts among institutions that can generate conflicting versions of social reality, and there are forms of journalistic narrative in which the role of institutions is less predominant. But, as sociologist Fishman notes, the way that facts are defined in journalism gives a high priority to bureaucratically generated accounts: "If reporters draw their own inferences from available accounts, they cannot report them as facts. If somebody else draws the inferences—and usually this somebody else is an official empowered to do so—then the journalist can treat the inferences as hard facts."[17]

Beat reporters orient their activity around the schedules and structures of institutions, thereby creating a public reality in which institutions are predominant actors. Inevitably, this must be at the expense of other content. Forms of social life that lack bureaucratic structures, spokespersons, and fact-generating machinery are not caught in the news net, except insofar as they interact with bureaucratic structures or adapt themselves to the requirements of the news-making apparatus.

This conception of the role of the media and the equation of objective reporting with the transmission of bureaucratically generated facts can be traced to Walter Lippmann and the Progressive movement, as we have seen in Chapter 3. Lippmann argued in *Public Opinion* that "The common interests in life very largely elude public opinion entirely and can be managed only by a specialized class whose personal interests reach beyond the locality."[18] Lippmann's conception helps us to understand how objective journalism has contributed to the decline of communities and the public sphere.

In the liberal view, as expressed by Lippmann, the rational critical discourse that must take place in order to make sound social policy can only take place within a coherent, rational, educated elite that shares a commitment (not shared by the broader public) to disinterested scientific inquiry. Within that framework, the news media have the responsibility of serving as a watchdog for the public and of explaining and securing public consent for elite policy and decisions. Within this conception, government is democratic if it operates with the consent of the governed. Lippmann's prescriptions gave journalistic practice an epistemological frame that interprets social reality in terms of institutions and individuals. The social structures of the informal or associational sector (that is, "family, friends, neighbors, neighborhood associations, clubs, civic groups, local enterprises, churches, ethnic associations, temples, local unions, local government and local media"[19]) were consequently marginalized.

What impact does this media depiction of social reality have on social reality? This question is a tricky one; as it is framed, it suggests that we can make a meaningful distinction between a "real world" and a mirror world constructed by the news media. It seems more correct to acknowledge that the boundary and distinction between direct and mediated experience has become hopelessly blurred. Many Americans spend 30 hours or more every week watching television, entering into long-term emotional relationships with television characters or personalities who may be real or fictional. Insofar as our sense of the "real" is grounded in shared experience, mediated experiences that are widely shared often have a stronger claim to reality than experiences that are direct but not shared.

Although it is true that much happens in the world that is not captured in journalistic accounts, it is predominantly the events that are captured by the news net, placed in an interpretive frame, and transmitted to a mass audience that have the potential for widespread impact. The news media provide a frame through which much of interpersonal experience can be interpreted. To the extent that we have a world to talk about with our neighbors, it is most often the world presented to us by the mass media.

The decline of the community and public sphere is widely attributed to the collapse of traditional social forms in the face of modernity. The late twentieth century has seen a widespread decline in civic institutions, ranging from the unraveling of neighborhoods and families to declining participation in more formally structured forms of voluntary civic organization such as churches, political parties, block clubs, and fraternal organizations.[20] It is perhaps no coincidence that the twentieth century has also seen an unprecedented blossoming of bureaucratic discourses and the proliferation of bureaucratically (and hierarchically) organized structures for the management of every dimension of social life: health care systems, welfare systems, systems for the management of the poor, the mentally ill, the socially deviant, and increasing rationalization of the organizational structures of businesses and educational institutions.

John McKnight argues that there is a direct link between the rise of bureaucratic structures and the decline of community in America:

> Whenever hierarchical systems become more powerful than the community, we see the flow of authority, resources, skills, dollars, legitimacy, and capaci-

ties away from communities to service systems. In fact, institutionalized systems grow at the expense of communities. As institutions gain power, communities lose their potency and the consent of community is replaced by the control of systems; the citizens of community are replaced by the clients and consumers of institutional products.[21]

Although this "increasing organization of everything" has been widely noted and analyzed, relatively little attention has been paid to the role of the news media in extending the reach of these power structures into the social body and into the construction of personal identity. This is not to say that bureaucratic institutions do not predate the rise of objective journalism (they predate it by centuries) or that the mass media are responsible for the creation of these institutions. But the social power of these institutions consists, at least in large part, in their ability to transmit their versions of reality, and this power is sustained in large part through the agency of the mass media.

The impact on public life has been profound. James Carey argues that "the public has been dissolved, in part, by journalism." More specifically, Carey maintains, the dissolution was caused by the sweeping changes in journalistic practice introduced by the institutionalization of objectivity. According to Carey, Lippmann believed that the proper role for journalists was to act as "symbolic brokers who translate the arcane language of experts into a publicly accessible language for the masses. They transmit the judgments of experts and thereby ratify decisions arrived at by that class— not by the public or public representatives." The consequence of this view has been, over the decades, a sweeping delegitimation of public discourse. "Lippmann, in effect, takes the public out of politics and politics out of public life."[22]

Lippmann did not completely deny the public a role in political life. Although the public were largely relegated to the role of spectators, they were spectators whose consent gave legitimacy to the established order and who held the power of the ballot box to remove leaders who failed to act in the public interest. But this role is distinctly limited (and limiting).

One of the most significant instances of the impact of the news media on social institutions has been the impact of television on the institutions of democracy, that is, on the way campaigns are run, issues are defined, and constituencies are built. Television has become the most significant medium for the transmission of political discourse and, thus, also for the public understanding of political discourse. Simultaneously, it has transformed that discourse: politicians now adapt their message to the medium by encapsulating their ideas into sound bites. The result, argues Robert Entman, has been a debasement of the political system: "Bluntly speaking, the media now provide an overwhelming temptation for politicians and other political figures to engage in demagoguery."[23]

The decline of the public sphere and traditional forms of civic engagement is sometimes discussed in terms that suggest a lost golden era. Revisionist historians such as Claude Fischer have questioned whether the ideal communities nostalgically evoked by contemporary communitarian theorists ever really existed. Fischer argues that the rosy visions of the past rest upon historically inaccurate pictures of places, such as New England, and eras, such as the 1950s, that were quite anomalous in important ways.[24] In a similar spirit, others have pointed out that the model of public discourse embodied in the coffee houses and political journals of the Enlightenment era was, like the Athenian model of participatory democracy, very restrictive in terms of who was allowed to participate.

Historically, the public "spaces" in which public discourse took place were initially the physical spaces of inns and coffee houses and the pages of the early partisan newspapers, which restricted participation to those with the requisite wealth and leisure time—that is, bourgeois men. The space of public discourse gradually expanded, though, to include the pages of the popular press, and the emergence of the penny newspapers made the public sphere accessible to a much broader public.

According to Benjamin Barber, Lippmann is part of a long tradition of political thought that sees a profound tension between participatory democracy on the one hand and liberal values such as autonomy, liberty, and tolerance on the other. "In each case, the charge is that democracy untempered by liberalism becomes distempered democracy, that popular government carries within itself a seed of totalitarian despotism."[25] The key question here is whether the greater danger lies in the threat posed by an "excess of democracy" to liberal values, as Lippmann would suggest, or in the threat posed to democracy by an excess of liberalism, as communitarian theorists such as Benjamin Barber, Mary Ann Glendon, and Harry Boyte argue.[26]

The Importance of Community and the Public Sphere

Even on its own terms, the information-centered model of objective journalism is a failure. If we set aside the fundamental question of whether the information transmitted by the media is properly regarded as constituting a factual representation of reality, the news media have still been less than successful at fulfilling their mission as defined by liberal democratic theory, that is, giving citizens the information they need to be active participants in self-governance. Not only has the rise of objective journalism been paralleled by a decline in citizen participation in public life, but numerous surveys of public knowledge show that very little of the information transmitted is actually received—or at least retained. Although the predominant model of an objective press emphasizes information at the expense of ideas or debate, surveys of the American public invariably show alarmingly low levels of basic knowledge about world events. Christopher Lasch argues that

> As things stand now, the press generates information in abundance, and nobody pays any attention. It is no secret that the public knows less about public affairs than it used to know. Millions of Americans cannot begin to tell you what is in the bill of rights, what Congress does, what the Constitution says about the powers of the presidency, how the party system emerged, or how it operates.[27]

The fact that most Americans cannot name their U.S. representative can't be explained in terms of a failure of the news media to report the activities of Congress. Rather, Lasch suggests, news consumers don't retain political news because they do not perceive themselves as having a meaningful role to play in the political process. Lasch argues that what democracy needs is public debate, not information. Of course, it needs information too, but the kind of information it needs can be generated only by vigorous popular debate. We do not know what we need to know until we ask the right questions, and we can identify the right questions only by subjecting our own ideas about the world to the test of public controversy.[28]

Some defenders of objective journalism may wish to argue that the decline of civic engagement and the decline of the public sphere are the price that we have to pay for progress. These social structures simply aren't capable of responding to the complex, technical problems that modern societies have to deal with, and though there may be some positive aspects of these more primitive social structures whose passing we will nostalgically mourn, we have entered a period of human history in which only the leadership of experts can enable us to deal with the challenges we face.

To this, it may be countered that hierarchical bureaucratic structures have also proven themselves incapable of responding to the complex technological problems of modern society. As John McKnight argues, our "correctional systems" consistently train people in crime. Studies demonstrate that a substantial number of people, while in hospital, become sick or injured with maladies worse than those for which they were admitted. In many of our big city schools we see children whose relative achievement levels fall farther behind every year.[29]

McKnight contends that this pattern of "crime-making correction systems, sickness-making health systems, and stupid-making schools" is the result of a social model that "conceives society as a place bounded by institutions and individuals." What is missing from this model, says McKnight, is the informal, associational sector. Although McKnight does not acknowledge the role of the news media in constructing this social model, it is the very model that has been institutionalized in journalism in this century through the procedural norms of objectivity.

According to McKnight, one reason why social planners ignore community is that "there are many institutional leaders who simply do not believe in the capacities of communities. They often see communities as collections of parochial, inexpert, uninformed and biased people."[30] This, of course, closely parallels Walter Lippmann's view of the public. Increasingly, as communities deteriorate, it becomes a self-fulfilling prophecy.

Harvard sociologist Robert Putnam speaks of the decline of civic engagement as a loss of social capital. Over the past generation, there has been a sharp decline in the level of civic participation in everything from church groups and fraternal organizations to the PTA. At the same time, the culture of cynicism within the press has undermined public faith in those bureaucratic institutions that are the central players in journalism's picture of reality. "Step by step," says James Fallows, "mainstream journalism has fallen into the habit of portraying public life in America as a race to the bottom, in which one group of conniving, insincere politicians ceaselessly tries to outmaneuver another."[31]

It doesn't seem farfetched to suggest a connection between this kind of depiction of the world of politics in the news media, and the declining public participation noted by Putnam:

> By almost every measure, Americans' direct engagement in politics and government has fallen steadily and sharply over the last generation, despite the fact that average levels of education—the best individual-level predictor of political participation—have risen sharply throughout this period. Every year over the last decade or two, millions more have withdrawn from the affairs of their communities.

Not coincidentally, Americans have also disengaged psychologically from politics and government over this era. The proportion of Americans who reply that they "trust the government in Washington" only "some of the time" or "almost never" has risen steadily from 30 percent in 1966 to 75 percent in 1992.[32]

The bureaucratic institutions that have become predominant in our way of life are increasingly unable to perform the basic functions that are the ultimate measure of any system of social organization: feeding the hungry, educating the young, healing the sick, and protecting our society's most vulnerable members. There is, Putnam has argued, a strong connection between how well government works and the vitality of civic life. Although journalism is far from the only factor that has contributed to the decline of civic life, it clearly has the potential to play a constructive role in rebuilding it.

7

Toward a Pragmatist Ethical Theory for Journalism

Journalism only makes sense in relation to the public and public life. Therefore, the fundamental problem in journalism is to reconstitute the public, to bring it back into existence.[1]

—James Carey

What philosophical foundations can the ethics of journalism rest on, if not on the doctrines of objectivity, neutrality, and the centrality of information? The answer may lie in the American philosophical tradition of pragmatism and in the work of John Dewey on problems of truth, communications, and society. John Dewey was one of Walter Lippmann's chief intellectual adversaries during the 1920s, when Lippmann was propounding his theory of democracy. Dewey did not disagree that individual citizens were on the whole poorly prepared to play an active role in democratic life, but he was far more optimistic than Lippmann about the potential of the public. Moreover, he argued, the government by experts that Lippmann proposed, with the public relegated to ratifying expert opinions, could never "be anything but an oligarchy managed in the interests of the few."[2] Only the public can truly say what the public good is, and that can only be discovered through public participation in an ongoing conversation.

Because communication was so central to Dewey's theory of democracy, he was keenly interested in the role of the press. When Dewey speaks of a public, he means a group of people who are affected by the indirect

129

consequences of the actions of others. Government arises out of the need to control those consequences in order to protect the public's interests. In a democracy, the members of the public participate to the fullest extent of their capacity in self-governance.

America's democratic institutions are the legacies of a less complex era. But unlike Lippmann, Dewey did not feel that the complexity of modern society made it necessary to abandon the ideal of participatory democracy. Rather, he believed that new forms of communication must be developed to make democratic participation possible in a more complex society. "Without such communication," Dewey wrote, "the public will remain shadowy and formless, seeking spasmodically for itself, but seizing and holding its shadow rather than its substance. Till the Great Society is converted into a Great Community, the public will remain in eclipse. Communication can alone create a great community."[3]

Dewey's philosophy seems particularly timely and relevant for journalism today. The vitality of public life was a major concern of Dewey's writing, and today it has become a central issue for many journalists.

Democracy and Public Participation

Dewey's concept of public opinion is rooted in an intellectual tradition that can be traced back to Montesquieu. In this tradition of thought, public opinion is understood as a body of shared beliefs and attitudes that emerged within the public sphere. With the decline of absolutism in the Renaissance, there emerged an independent social sphere, dominated by neither church nor monarch, in which an educated class was able to meet, to exchange ideas, and to formulate improved, shared concepts to benefit society as a whole. The venues for this discourse were neither churches nor the royal courts, but salons, coffee houses, and the pages of the early newspapers, which offered both a forum for ideas and a stimulus for face-to-face discussion. The public itself can thus be seen as in some sense a product of the media. It was the early newspapers that provided a common body of knowledge and ideas among urban residents who were not connected by face-to-face relationships.

The participants in this discourse saw themselves as citizens, not merely giving expression to private interests, but rather participating as representatives of the larger society. Public opinion, as understood in this tradition, was the social consensus that emerged as the result of dialogue. Juergen Habermas traces the decline of the public sphere to the middle of the last century, prompted by, among other factors, the transformation of newspapers from political journals into commercial enterprises, and the development of a broader, more heterogeneous audience.[4]

A great deal has been written about the decline of the public and the decline of community. Both issues are complex, but they are distinct. What is meant by community seems generally to be small groups "bound together by history, faith, and fellowship." The notion of a public, by contrast, is that of private individuals, who do not necessarily share a common history, faith, or fellowship, but who come together to participate in critical rational discourse about common concerns on the basis of common knowledge—a common knowledge provided by shared sources of information.

The concern with revitalizing the public sphere goes back at least to the 1920s, when John Dewey worried, in *The Public and Its Problems*, about the eclipse of the public. Recently, there has been a major upsurge of interest in revitalizing the public sphere, evidenced by such works as *The Good Society* by Robert Bellah, Richard Madsen, William Sullivan, Ann Swidler, and Steven Tipton; Benjamin Barber's *Strong Democracy*; and such civic enterprises as Harry Boyte's Project Public Life and Frances Moore Lappe's Center for Living Democracy, as well as the writings of Jay Rosen, James Carey, Noam Chomsky, and Douglas Kellner.

Is Participatory Democracy Desirable?

Any defender of participatory democracy must address the objection that, as Benjamin Barber phrases it, "popular government carries within it the seeds of a totalitarian despotism."[5] John Dewey's answer is, in part, that if the people cannot be trusted to take an active role in governing themselves, then it is not plausible to imagine that they can play a meaningful role as watchdogs over their leaders either. The real alternative, in this view, is not elite democracy, but oligarchy. And, argues Dewey, "the world has suffered more from leaders and authorities than from the masses." Dewey was prepared to acknowledge that the average citizen, considered as an individual, does lack the knowledge necessary to play an effective role in governing. But for Dewey, it was not the individual in isolation who was to play an active role in self-governance; it was the individual as the member of a community and as a participant in the processes of debate and discussion who had the ability to draw on the knowledge of others and participate in the formation of a public will.

Nonetheless, our collective memory is haunted by images of masses out of control: lynchings and pogroms and the mass terrorism of a Kristallnacht. But are these really examples of publics that have become overly active, as social conservatives and political realists would argue, or masses of individuals who have become overly passive, as advocates of participatory democracy maintain? Barber argues that "thin democracy has itself nourished some of the pathologies that it has attributed to direct democracy and . . . strong democracy may offer remedies for the very diseases it has been thought to occasion."[6]

The frenzied masses feared by democratic realists are most frequently seen in totalitarian or oligarchic societies, and their participants typically have little access to effective mechanisms of democratic participation. By contrast, the very culture of democratic participation fosters a climate of rationality, deliberation, and respect for persons. In participatory democracies, by definition, power and decision-making authority is decentralized and diffused throughout the society. The capacity for collective will-formation at the smallest levels of organization is enhanced, but the capacity for the formation of a mass will is diminished.

In the past few years, the theoretical debate between democratic realists and advocates of strong or participatory democracy has been overtaken by events. There has been a devolution of power from the federal to the state and local levels, and a scaling back of our national commitment to provide, through the mechanisms of government, basic social guarantees in the areas of education, housing, welfare, and other social services. The responsibility for addressing these needs is being shifted to communities and individuals. With a change in the political reality of who must govern and solve problems comes a change in the institutional definitions of who and what is newsworthy. The Lippmann model of the citizen as interested spectator must be abandoned as citizens become the key players in the social drama.

Is Participatory Democracy Possible?

Some social critics, such as British sociologist John Thompson, question the viability of participatory democracy in a mass media age. The arguments raised by Thompson against the ideal of public participation have less to do with a distrust of the public than with considerations related to technology and scale. Thompson argues that "the idea of the public sphere is largely inapplicable to the circumstances of the late twentieth century," and he offers two arguments for this claim:

1. . . . The development of technical media has dramatically altered the nature of mass communications and the conditions under which it takes place, so much so that the original idea of the public sphere could not simply be reactivated on a new footing. The media of print have increasingly given way to electronically mediated forms of mass communication, and especially television, and these new media have transformed the very conditions of interaction, communication and information diffusion in modern societies.

2. The second reason why the idea of the public sphere is of limited relevance today is that the idea is linked fundamentally to a notion of participatory opinion formation. The idea of the public sphere assumes that the personal opinions of individuals will become *public opinion* through, and only through participation in a free and equal debate which is open in principle to all. But this assumption, whatever relevance it may have had to eighteenth-century political life (and this may have been considerably less than Habermas suggests) is far removed from the political realities and possibilities of the twentieth century. . . . We live in a world today in which the sheer scale and complexity of decision-making processes limits the extent to which they can be organized in a participatory way. Hence the original idea of the public sphere, in so far as it is linked to the idea of participatory opinion formation, is of limited relevance today.[7]

Neither of these objections seems fatal. If we understand the public sphere as an ideal, realized only in a very partial way even in the Enlightenment, then the prospect of even a partial realization of this ideal in our own era may seem like a partial victory worth striving for, rather than a dream impossible to achieve.

The emergence of new media makes participation more, rather than less possible. It is not face-to-face participation that matters, but rather participation in dialogue, and new technologies have broadened the possibilities for public participation. However imperfectly realized, such new forms of media as talk radio and electronic bulletin boards offer new forums for public dialogue. Their potential to serve the common good can only increase if civility is acknowledged as a core value for public communicators. Public access channels on cable television are as yet little used, but they too represent a space in which public dialogue can take place. Although it is true that some decision-making takes place on a scale that makes public participation difficult or impossible, that would seem to constitute an argument for, rather than against, political decentralization. Even though some decision-making must take place on a regional, national, or even international scale, there is also a great deal of decision-making that takes place on a local scale and can be opened up to much greater participation.

Outlines of an Ethical Theory

An ethical theory grounded in the philosophical tradition of pragmatism offers the news media a much more promising means of fulfilling the social role envisioned for them by democratic theory, that is, enabling citizens to play an active role in self-governance. Ultimately, these principles and practices may also provide a way for journalists to find in daily practice a fulfillment of the ideals of public service that attracted many of them to journalism.

It may be helpful to summarize the key elements of the realist/objectivist view embodied in traditional journalism ethics and then contrast them with the pragmatist view.

Ontology

In the traditional realist view, the world exists independently of our knowledge of it, and there are facts about the world that are true, independent of any human knowledge of them. In the pragmatist view, reality is socially constructed, emerging out of the human activity of creating words and concepts as tools to meet human needs. The concepts and categories through which we try to understand and manipulate our environment emerge historically as the products of human interaction with each other and with our environment. As we transform our social reality through our productive activity, we continuously transform our language and the concepts and categories through which we see the world.

Epistemology

In the realist view, truth consists in a correspondence between a statement and an external reality. By the use of scientific methods—or the scientifically based methods of journalistic objectivity—trained observers can come to have knowledge of the world that is objectively true. Expressions of fact must be clearly distinguished from expressions of opinion, which convey beliefs about facts for which we lack sufficient evidence, and from expressions of value, which state attitudes towards the facts.

The current role of the news media is to disseminate the vocabulary and the point of view of those segments of society that are recognized as authorized knowers. Insofar as the ethic of objectivity explicitly defined the news media as a medium for the transmission of an expert discourse, the structure of journalistic communication is designed to guarantee that the flow of vocabulary is overwhelmingly one-way. Journalists interview experts and then transmit their views to the public, but journalists generally do not disseminate "uninformed" public opinion.

In the pragmatist view, by contrast, a statement is true when its truth conditions are satisfied, but what these truth conditions may be is established through human activity. This conception of truth was expressed by William James when he defined truth as "what it is good for us to believe." What it is good for us to believe is established experientially: the criteria for what it is good for us to believe about how to bake bread bear no direct logical relation to what it is good for us to believe about the existence of an afterlife. The procedures known as "scientific method" or "journalistic objectivity" are just particular ways of interpreting the world; any special claim that they confer to epistemic authority must rest on their usefulness to particular human ends. Standards of truth and falsity are always internal to a domain of activity.

Some have suggested that this notion of truth invites relativism or even nihilism. Christopher Norris, for example, bitterly attacks the neopragmatism of Richard Rorty, Stanley Fish, and others as leading to a moral bankruptcy that easily rationalizes accommodation to power.[8] This consequence would indeed seem to follow from a notion that holds that multiple domains of activity (or communities of interpretation) entail multiple truths. But within the pragmatist conception, truth is always provisional, subject to revision in the light of new experience, changing values, or the encounter with other communities of interpretation.

If we wish to imagine a kind of truth that is not provisional, it could reside only in the kind of knowledge that would emerge at the end of all such experiments and encounters. Thus, C. S. Peirce describes truth as "the opinion which is fated to be ultimately agreed to by all who investigate."[9] This notion of ultimate truth seems problematic; why suppose that all who investigate will ever reach agreement? Even if one remains agnostic about whether such ultimate consensus is possible, Peirce's description points to several features of a pragmatist conception of truth that are more widely shared: understanding truth as a product of human activity, and specifically, as the product of a social, rather than individual process of inquiry. This pragmatist notion of truth seems to be compatible with Habermas' notion that universal consensus under ideal conditions is the criterion of defensible truth claims. The ideal conditions that Habermas envisions are characterized by uncoerced and equal participation in public discourse.

What are the practical implications of the rejection of journalistic objectivity? The rejection of objectivity consists not merely in the assertion that the news media fail to provide an objective picture of reality, or even that objectivity is impossible in practice, but rather that it is impossible even in theory. There is no neutral standpoint from which we can give an account of reality that is a-perspectival. Denying that there is such a thing as objective truth is not denying that there is such a thing as truth; nor is it saying that all truth claims are of equivalent value. Rather, it is to say that propositions are always true or false relative to some standard that is internal to a theory, language game, or system of beliefs.

One implication of this conceptualization is that journalists should continuously try to explore and to disclose the frame of reference and the conscious and hidden assumptions from within which they and their sources operate. This is a responsibility for journalists to a far greater degree than for practitioners of other disciplines or professions precisely because journalism is not a discipline in which standards of truth and fundamental premises are established by convention and are relatively stable. Journalism operates in a public sphere in which multiple standards and interpretations come into conflict. Another implication is that the provisional and contestable character of truth claims should be emphasized; where there is significant disagreement, the media should be made accessible to and should disseminate the widest possible range of viewpoints.

Social Role

In the realist view, the primary social function of the news media is the collecting, organizing, and disseminating of information. In order to perform these functions effectively (as observer, gatekeeper, and messenger), the news media must maintain a stance of neutrality and avoid becoming instigators or participants in the events that they cover.

In the pragmatist view, the media of mass communications are one of the most important institutions through which we come to know ourselves as individuals and as members of society. Our common language and values are circulated by the mass media; within the mass media, the news media play a particular role in defining the set of common understandings and values that sustain the social order. The challenge is to perform that role fairly, in a way that addresses not merely individual interests, but also the common interest that defines us as a public.

Ethics

In the realist view, the primary duty of the news media is to give a true picture of the world that can serve as the basis for political participation. Within this view, theorists disagree about the degree of public participation that is possible or desirable. Whereas social responsibility theorists, such as the authors of the Hutchins Commission report, envision active participation in self-governance, democratic realists like Lippmann favor a more limited role for the public—namely the ratification of expert decisions. From this ontology, epistemology, and conception of the social roles of the news media is derived the set of values previously discussed: accuracy, fairness, objectivity, truth-telling, avoidance of conflict of interest, and so on. We have seen, though, that this derivation is powerfully influenced by the relations of power within the news media.

In the pragmatist view—or at least in this version of pragmatism—there can be no such thing as the one true picture of the world. Rather, we are all continuously in the process of constructing and modifying our pictures in light of new experiences and changing objectives. As individuals, we have the capacity to make use of the experiences of others in modifying our pictures of reality and redefining our objectives. As members of communities, we operate most successfully when a broad range of perceptions and values enters into our deliberations.

From this pragmatist perspective, the proper role of the news media is to facilitate the operation of communities as contexts for democratic decision-making. This means that journalism must serve as a medium for the public exchange of ideas and for the exchange of competing views of reality and the public good; in addition, it should facilitate the formation of public consensus. The arguments that follow rest upon a view of the ideal social order as one in which all citizens participate, to the limits of their abilities, in determining the course of their common life. Towards that end, the key values of the news media must include accessibility, respect for persons, fairness, interpretation, and skepticism.

Professional Principles

It probably would not be helpful to propose a revised code of ethics for journalists. Traditionally, at least, such codes are part of the ideology of professionalism and have sustained the idea that journalism is properly the domain of a specialized class. What is needed instead is to open up the process of news making and to create new forms of partnership between news producers and news consumers.

This does not mean a wholesale abandonment of the principles expressed in current codes of professional ethics. Objectivity, both as a procedural norm and as an epistemological objective, must be rejected, but such values as accuracy, fairness, and the injunction to avoid sensationalism remain important. The injunction to avoid conflict of interest gives way to an obligation to fully disclose interests and to give access to a broad spectrum of interests. All of these values become subject to reinterpretation in the context of a pragmatist conception of the role of the news media in public life.

As with the prevailing liberal/realist model, a pragmatist theory of journalistic responsibility would take as its foundation a commitment to enable citizens to participate in democratic life, though with a much more robust conception of what participation means. But a pragmatist account would regard not the transmission of information, but rather the creation and sustaining of a public sphere as the most important role of journalism in a democratic society.

This difference in conception of the social role of the news media implies a different set of professional principles:

- *Diversity and Accessibility.* Democracy is equated with the widest possible participation of citizens in public life, and thus one of the foundational professional commitments must be to diversity and accessibility. Journalists must actively seek to make sure that the widest possible range of viewpoints is represented in public debate.
- *Civility.* Another core value in the promotion of civic life must be civility, a set of behavioral norms built around the idea of respect for persons. The media are the most important sources for the ideas the public has about how conflicts, and especially conflicts between strangers, are resolved. Since the media have traditionally placed a priority on dramatically charged images of conflict and confrontation, there has been little symbolic representation of how peace-making, reconciliation, and compromise are achieved.
- *Debate and Dialogue.* Since facts are understood not as accurate representations of reality, but rather as interpretations of reality from a point of view, the greatest emphasis must be given to those issues in public life where there are significant divergences of interpretation. Specifically, the news media ought to serve as a forum for debate and

dialogue. Whether there was an earthquake in Azerbaijan is not a matter over which there is much divergence in interpretation, nor is it a matter of much immediate consequence for the lives of most American news consumers; by contrast, whether the United States should give large-scale foreign aid to the states that made up the former Soviet Union is a matter of far greater consequence to American citizens and a subject over which there is much greater disagreement.

With the acknowledgment that the news media do make the news and are inevitably major players on the social stage, the news media can begin to openly engage the question of how their social responsibilities are to be fulfilled. The pragmatist conception of the social responsibility of the news media understands participation and democracy in much more robust terms than does the objectivist account. Democracy, in a Deweyan view, requires the active participation of all citizens, to the limits of their ability, in determining the course of the common life. This concept of democracy extends its meaning beyond the political sphere to the workplace, home, and school. Participation means that each individual has an opportunity not merely to give assent, but to be heard.

This conception of democracy poses a problem of scale: although the New England town meeting was small enough that each citizen could be heard, the modern city is far too large to accommodate such forms of direct democracy. The solution is, at least in part, that the citizen can participate through a variety of mediating institutions, such as precinct caucuses, block clubs, parent teacher associations, unions, or worker-management committees.

The role of the media in this expanded conception of democratic life is to facilitate and to model such participation. The media must serve as a forum for dialogue, not simply between individuals, but also between communities within a larger society. More fundamentally, they can enable individuals to find an identity as members of communities, to help members of communities communicate amongst themselves, to facilitate communication between communities, and to help communities find commonalities that link them as members of a greater community.

In practical terms, this expanded role can take a variety of forms, all of which suggest a redefinition of what counts as newsworthy. One form entails a greatly increased emphasis on the bulletin-board function: a great deal more space could be given over to announcements of meeting times, places, and agendas of civic organizations. The news media must also ensure that the citizen exists in the symbolic universe that it projects. The forms and norms of citizen participation can be modeled and communicated by the media, for example, in debates and discussions and in coverage of demonstrations or other forms of symbolic expression that emphasizes explanation.

The exclusion of the public from public debate that resulted from the rise of objectivity has had an impact on how individual citizens perceive themselves and their abilities. In large part, they do not perceive themselves as citizens at all, and they have little experience in the civic arts of debate. Moreover, they often do not perceive themselves as legitimate participants in public discourse. Beyond the implications these perceptions have for the larger society, on an individual level it reflects how establishing an expert discourse in the news media has resulted in a diminished selfhood for news consumers.

Whatever we want to see as a dynamic element of social reality must also have symbolic existence in the representation of reality constructed by news media. This implies a commitment to representing not only all communities within society, but also all of the occupations. The invisibility of, for example, service occupations in the mass media is a form of symbolic annihilation that devalues and demeans caretaking work and the people who perform it. If this society values the necessary work of teaching, childcare, nursing, and farming, the only meaningful expression of that value is in assuring that the symbolic representation of those activities reflects that valuation.

Moreover, many consumers of news media turn to newspapers and especially to television for the sense of belonging or community that the media create. This is often a false sense of community, argues Elayne Rapping, created by "happy family" news teams. But there is no reason to believe that many viewers would not be receptive to a more substantial concept of community.

The dogma of objectivity, or representation, privileges overt events at the expense of ideas, debates, or other forms of communication. A rejection of objectivity frees the news media from the commitment to the primacy of "news" and opens the door to other forms of journalism. A parents' guide to getting the most out of the public schools or an article on how to be a citizen-lobbyist do not qualify as news under any traditional definition, but they are examples of ways in which journalists can facilitate public participation.

8

Toward a Public Journalism

Putting forth a new theory of journalism ethics is easy, but probably not very useful. Others more diligent have put forward elaborate and closely reasoned theories that sometimes read as though they were written for a world slightly different from the one we live in, a world in which all agree to set aside their positions and their vested interests and let the best argument carry the day.

In the world we live in, what matters more than the ethical theory itself is how the theory is translated into practice, and as we have seen, that translation is likely to be shaped by relations of power and institutional interests. As the balance of power shifts away from journalists operating out of a professional ethos toward owners and managers who see the news business as a business, the possibility of a meaningful institutional conversation about journalism ethics becomes increasingly remote.

It is neither realistic nor desirable to merely call for a restoration of the crumbling wall that theoretically once separated the newsroom from the business office. In a market-driven environment, appeals to the sense of public responsibility of corporate owners or managers are likely to have limited impact. And restoring that wall would, of itself, do little to repair a more serious rupture: the loss of connection between journalists and the public.

The most fruitful work in the field of journalism ethics is therefore likely to be not in the area of abstract moral theory, but in the area of politics: creating an alliance between journalists and the public. Journalism cannot exist without a public, the public cannot come to know itself or defend its interests without journalists, and no productive conversation about the ethics of journalism can take place unless journalists and citizens alike have a place at the table. But one of the greatest obstacles to such an alliance is journalists' traditional stance of detachment.

A new movement has arisen in the American newspaper world explicitly acknowledging that newspapers must find ways to reconnect with their readers and must help their readers find ways to reconnect to public life. The beginnings of this movement, called public journalism or civic journalism, can be traced to the late 1980s, when several newspapers around the country began to search for ways of refocusing their coverage of politics and community affairs to make it more relevant to their readers.

In 1988, the *Columbus, Georgia, Ledger-Enquirer* published a six-part series called "Columbus Beyond 2000" which examined, in depth, the serious challenges facing the community. When the series failed to have any impact on local government or public life, the newspaper's executive editor decided to go one step further. The paper organized a town meeting and then helped create a new civic organization, United Beyond 2000, which pulled together task forces to address specific problems such as race relations and health care.

In 1990, Davis "Buzz" Merritt, editor of the *Wichita Eagle,* decided to take a new approach to covering the upcoming elections: surveys and focus groups were used to determine which issues were of the greatest concern to readers. Instead of simply covering the candidates' speeches and attacks on each other, the newspaper began to actively press the candidates to address those public concerns. Two years later, the *Eagle* launched The People Project: Solving It Ourselves, which focused on how ordinary citizens could actively participate in solving problems in their communities.

One of the most famous of the poll-driven experiments in public journalism was conducted by North Carolina's *Charlotte Observer,* which polled 1,000 area residents about their greatest concerns in the 1992 election campaigns and then published a list of these concerns, which it identified as the Citizens Agenda. Editor Rich Oppel announced the new approach with a front-page column titled "We'll Help You Regain Control of the Issues." Instead of posing their own questions to the candidates, reporters asked questions forwarded by readers. When a candidate declined to answer some of the questions from the public, Oppel threatened to print the question anyway, with a blank space to indicate the candidate's noncompliance.

Jay Rosen, a professor of journalism at New York University, took note of these experiments and began to articulate a philosophical rationale for this new approach to journalism. Rosen has also played a central role in transforming a set of scattered experiments into a coherent movement; with a grant from the Knight Foundation and support from the Kettering

Foundation, he created the Project on Public Life and the Press, which brings together journalists to share ideas and publicize efforts at public journalism. Although Rosen maintains that public journalism is too rich and evolving a concept to be adequately captured by a definition, he has reluctantly offered the following formulation:

> Public journalism is an approach to the daily business of the craft that calls on journalists to: (1) address people as citizens, potential participants in public affairs, rather than victims or spectators; (2) help the political community act upon, rather than just learn about, its problems; (3) improve the climate of public discussion, rather than simply watch it deteriorate; and (4) help make public life go well, so that it earns its claim on our attention.[1]

While the public journalism movement shares with traditional objective journalism a commitment to enabling citizens to participate more fully in democratic life, it also recognizes that the news media are not, and cannot be, neutral observers. Rather, the public journalist seeks to be, in the words of *Wichita Eagle* Editor Merritt, "a fair-minded participant" in the life of the community.

The public journalism movement has caused considerable controversy within journalism. Although some have embraced it, others have sharply criticized it, arguing that when journalists abandon their role as observers and become participants or advocates, they compromise both their impartiality and their credibility. Support has generally been stronger from top editors and newspaper executives than from rank-and-file journalists, who are frequently very skeptical. In part, this skepticism comes out of a commitment to a traditional, objectivity-based conception of the journalist's role. But it may also be fueled by the deep distrust—and often bitterness—that many journalists feel about the culture change taking place at newspapers around the country. They believe that management's dismantling of the wall between journalistic and corporate culture and embracing of market-driven journalism represent both a threat to their autonomy and status as professionals and an abandonment of the newspaper's responsibilities to the community. When management embraces the vocabulary of community-"connectedness" or "public journalism"—the cynicism that the staff feels about the new management rhetoric (whether it is about promoting empowerment or public dialogue) extends to any efforts at public journalism—especially if management is pushing that shift in philosophy.

The public journalism movement may be journalism's last best hope, but whether it fulfills its promise will depend on how its stated principles are translated into practice. A truly public journalism may help to rebuild trust between the public and the press, but if, as many journalists fear, public journalism becomes merely a marketing strategy, it will only deepen public cynicism.

What public journalism will come to mean in practice depends in large part on how several key terms are interpreted. "Reconnecting with readers" can be taken to mean developing a relationship in which journalists and ordinary citizens enter into a conversation about the needs of the community and the needs of readers as citizens. Or it can be taken as a rationale for moving from the traditional model in which the journalist makes expert judgments about what the reader needs to know to a model in which content decisions are driven by market research about readers' interests. Similarly, enabling citizens to become more effective participants in democratic life can be understood either as enabling citizens to make better decisions at the ballot box or in terms of a more robust conception of democratic participation.

There are several useful distinctions that can be made regarding public journalism: between approaches that emphasize public deliberation and those that emphasize community involvement; between approaches that focus on projects and those that integrate the values of public journalism into newsroom routines; and between approaches that see public journalism as journalism *about* the public and those that see it as journalism *with* the public.

Projects that emphasize deliberation can take two forms—one inspired by the model of participatory democracy and the other inspired by representative democracy. To a degree, the different models can also be linked to different conceptions of truth: one seeks to create a picture of public opinion that corresponds to the way things really are (what the public "really" thinks), while the other sees public deliberation as a tool in the pursuit of truth—a more pragmatist conception of truth—that emerges through deliberation.

Public Journalism as Journalism About the Public

Journalism *about* the public aims to revitalize a vision of citizenship that has been dominant in American politics for most of this century—one in which citizens are (in Walter Lippmann's term) "interested spectators of action." In this vision of democracy, the primary role of citizens, apart from paying taxes, is to vote and, by extension, to remain sufficiently informed about the issues that they can cast an informed ballot. Although it does not significantly redefine either newsroom routines or the relationship between journalists and citizens, it modifies traditional practice by incorporating more voices of non-experts into stories about public issues and by relying more heavily on polling and focus groups to guide coverage.

Peter Parisi, professor of journalism and mass communication at Hunter College of the City University of New York, cautions that allowing polling to set the journalist's agenda is an evasion of the journalist's responsibility, not unlike the evasion that more traditional journalists effect through their reliance on official sources. "Civic journalists have put the local community in place of officials, but are running away from their role as defining and informing moderators of the discussion of social values," he argues.[2] The danger in letting community opinion drive the news agenda, according to Parisi, is that the public may not be the best judge of which social issues are most pressing or how those issues should be framed.

This approach to public journalism tends to focus on electoral politics and on public opinion as measured by polls. Its proponents may convene panels of representative citizens to deliberate about legislative issues. Journalism *about* the public is certainly an improvement over journalism *without* the public— that is, journalism that only follows the horse race or that covers politics as an insiders' game. But at a time when so many citizens have turned away from the electoral process, this approach may not be sufficient to re-engage readers as citizens, even in the limited role of spectators, or to reconnect them to their newspaper. Although studies of several public journalism projects have found that they were at least moderately successful in promoting public engagement, a recent public journalism experiment conducted by the *Hackensack, New Jersey, Record* with support from the Pew Center for Civic Journalism found that a massive commitment of resources to issues-focused coverage of the 1996 New Jersey Senate race made virtually no impression on readers. Among the explanations for the failure of the project cited by the authors of a summary report: "Finally, it may be that the public is not sufficiently interested in politics for public journalism to be of service."[3]

Using polling to drive campaign coverage has other pitfalls, illustrated by North Carolina's 1996 Senate race. When a consortium of North Carolina newspapers and radio and television stations joined together to create the Your Voice, Your Vote consortium, they decided to focus their coverage of the campaign on four of the eight issues determined by their polling to be foremost in the voters' minds. One issue they opted to discard was "Families and Values," which happened to be the key issue on which Senator Jesse Helms ran his campaign. Michael Kelly, in a scathing account of the project in the *New Yorker* magazine, remarks that "The consortium in effect decided that this year Helms wasn't running on those values at all, but rather, on the values it approved of."[4] (Defenders of the project have responded that it made up only a small part of the total coverage the participating media gave to the race.)

One frequently used model typically begins with telephone polling to elicit the issues of greatest concern to the public. The next step, quantifying the data, often leaves little room for nuance; each issue is reduced to a phrase or even a single word, such as "crime and drugs," "taxes and spending," or "education." What is not clear is whether the resulting list really indicates public concerns or merely reflects relative amounts of attention accorded to these topics by the media. One legacy of objectivity is the journalist's own belief that he or she has thereby produced a picture of a greater reality—of "what citizens really care about." But it is unclear whether the respondents, who may have little or no sense of themselves as citizens, really care about these issues or whether these are merely the issues that they know they should care about.

The group that is then brought together to discuss the issues can hardly be said to constitute a public; they are a collection of strangers, often from very different communities, who may not see each other again after this encounter and who have not had the opportunity to develop the relationships of trust and understanding that are essential to democratic cooperation. It is also unclear whether the conversation that follows can be considered true deliberation.

Daniel Yankelovich has described seven stages that public deliberation must go through in reaching the final stage of public judgment;[5] when it is the nation as a whole that engages in a dialogue about key issues such as civil rights, the process can take years. Social scientists such as James Fishkin and organizations such as the Kettering Foundation, the Study Circle Resource Center, and the Jefferson Center for New Democratic Process have developed methods, ranging from Fishkin's deliberative polling to study circles and citizen juries, that are designed to facilitate and accelerate this deliberative process so that it can be carried out in a matter of weeks or even days. In some newspaper-sponsored forums, the conversation may take place in as little as 90 minutes, during which time a problem is posed, participants are given an opportunity to describe their own personal experience with the issue at hand, various alternative solutions to the problem are explored, and a facilitator wraps up the discussion with a search for common ground. Rather than true deliberation, this sort of conversation is a simulacrum.

There may be real value to these kinds of conversations when they are part of an ongoing process of community-building and address problems at a level at which the community can actually take effective action. But when they are organized as one-time events and address, for example, national issues, they are unlikely to attract significant readership or response. They meet neither the traditional standards of newsworthiness, since they are about a pseudo-event featuring the opinions of non-experts, nor public journalism's standards of newsworthiness, since they offer neither tools or meaningful solutions.

One confusion at the heart of this approach to public journalism is whether the goal of deliberation is to produce ideas or data. In some versions, participants are surveyed before and after to see whether the conversations result in a change in attitudes. If the research goal is to compare percentages who favor A versus B before and after the deliberations, then the focus of the reporting is going to be on the possibilities defined at the onset of the conversation, rather than on any new ideas or common ground that may emerge from the process. And that misses the point of public deliberation.

Polling translates something complicated and amorphous—people's feelings and beliefs—into something tangible and concrete that journalists know how to deal with—a number, a fact, or a pie chart. It thereby circumvents the real challenge of listening to the public, that of discovering what people mean when they say that crime or the economy is their greatest concern or why they favor or oppose prayer in the schools.

But the most serious flaw in this approach to public journalism is that it does little to actually enhance the vitality of public life. A few selected citizens may be given a symbolic role in the political process, but the vast majority of citizens remain outsiders, looking in. Once the citizen forum is over, all the participants are paid their honoraria, and everybody goes home. This kind of public journalism leaves little or nothing behind. No change has been brought about, no new public space has been created, few if any new relationships have been established, and readers have been given no new resources for participating in public life or holding their public officials accountable. Nor, for that matter, have they been given any new resources for holding journalists accountable.

This approach to public journalism rests on three key equations: it equates the public with the collection of individuals who make up the populace; it equates public opinion with the aggregate of individual opinions, and it equates democracy with electoral politics. That approach is unlikely to reconstitute the public or to overcome the alienation of the public from journalism and politics. The only kind of public journalism that can accomplish those ends is one that starts with a more robust understanding of the public, public opinion, and democracy—one that offers the public more effective ways to participate in public life and to hold their elected representatives and the news media accountable.

A Richer Conception of Democracy

John Dewey had a much richer conception of the public, public opinion, and democracy, and he was forceful in emphasizing that the ideal of democracy was not to be confused with the apparatus that could be assembled to implement the ideal:

> The idea of democracy is a wider and fuller idea than can be exemplified in the state even at its best. To be realized it must affect all modes of human association, the family, the school, industry, religion. And even as far as political arrangements are concerned, governmental institutions are but a mechanism for securing to an idea channels of effective operation.[6]

Dewey offers an account of this "wider and fuller idea" both from the perspective of the individual and from the standpoint of the social groups within which individuals find their roles and identity:

> From the standpoint of the individual, it consists in having a responsible share according to capacity in forming and directing the activities of the groups to which one belongs and in participating according to need in the values which the groups sustain. From the standpoint of the groups, it demands liberation of potentialities of members of a group in harmony with the interests and goods which are common.[7]

This conception of democracy entails a much more active level of participation than merely paying taxes and voting. It entails being—to the degree that one is able—a participant in an ongoing conversation of one's community, a conversation that articulates differences and shared values and determines the direction of the common life.

For Dewey and the sociological tradition he influenced so strongly, "public" means more than a collection of individuals within a geographically defined area, and "public opinion" refers to something more than the responses elicited by opinion polls:

Unless there are methods for detecting the energies which are at work and tracing them through an intricate network of interactions to their consequences, what passes as public opinion will be "opinion" in its derogatory sense rather than truly public, no matter how widespread the opinion is. The number who share error as to fact and who partake of a false belief measures power for harm. Opinion casually formed and formed under the direction of those who have something at stake in having a lie believed can be *public* opinion only in name.

Calling it by this name, acceptance of the name as a kind of warrant, magnifies its capacity to lead action astray.[8]

In a democracy, as Dewey conceived it, the actions of the group are the product of the public will. But since the will of the public can only emerge as the product of public deliberation, then policies that are the product only of public consent, without deliberation or understanding, cannot be said to have been achieved democratically. Where genuine dialogue occurs, there is a weaving of competing perspectives towards a coherent whole, though it is a weaving that never reaches completion. The whole itself will reflect a perspective—that is, the perspective of the community—and the views of individual participants will reflect the transformation that they undergo in the course of participating in this dialogue.

Putting Pragmatist Values into Practice: Public Journalism as Journalism with the Public

The other possible direction is for public journalism to become journalism *with* the public—that is, journalism that engages citizens as active partners in the newsmaking process and makes itself a tool that enhances citizens' abilities to work together to solve common problems or to achieve common goals. Such an approach requires journalists to abandon their traditional stance of detachment and make themselves accountable to the communities they serve.

Journalism *with* the public can take a variety of forms. At the heart of this approach, though, is a very different kind of listening than journalists have traditionally practiced—public listening. Public listening involves not only listening to a much broader range of voices, but also listening in a different way. Traditionally, the journalistic interview is a kind of interrogation; the reporter asks the questions, and the interviewee supplies the answers. When naive interviewees try to take the conversation in a direction other than the reporter's line of inquiry, the reporter typically ignores the effort and steers the conversation back on track. What the reporter is looking for is, at worst, as Christopher Lasch lamented, a predetermined sound bite; even at best, it is usually specific data or a good quote. The essential form of the conversation is subject-object.

True public listening involves a more open-ended conversation and a greater degree of mutuality. The interview becomes a conversation that is not only a vehicle for the reporter to get the story, but also a way for the interviewees to tell theirs. One purpose of public listening is to enable the reporter to frame the story so that it captures what is at stake in the issue, not from the viewpoint of the "reasonable reader," but from the differing viewpoints of different stakeholders.

Journalism with the public can involve using the resources of the newspaper to encourage and support open public conversations at study circles, neighborhood roundtables, or public forums. One example of this approach is the We the People Project, a partnership between the *Wisconsin State Journal* of Madison, Wisconsin Public Radio, Wisconsin Public Television, and CBS affiliate WISC-TV. Since its founding in 1994, We the People has organized public forums and town hall meetings on health care, crime, the state budget, and statewide electoral contests. The Pew Charitable Trust, which has provided some funding for the project, had outside evaluators assess the success of the project. They found that We the People has had a positive impact on public life. Citizens aware of the project reported that it made them think more about politics (62 percent) and "made them want to be more involved in making Madison a better place to live" (64 percent).[9]

One criticism of this model is that its participants may not accurately represent the makeup of the larger community. In the case of a similar public discussion project, Minnesota's Talking, conducted by this author at the *Minneapolis–St. Paul Star Tribune* from 1992 to 1994, participants tended to be better educated, more affluent, more "civic-minded," more white, and perhaps more liberal than the population as a whole. But the cogency of this criticism depends on whether the goal of such projects is understood in terms of fostering public conversation or in terms of gathering data that accurately reflects "what the public really thinks."

A more significant criticism of these deliberation-centered projects is that deliberation is not enough. For public discussion to make a difference, the political system has to be responsive. To encourage the public to participate in public discussion in a context where there is little prospect that the conversation will have an impact runs the risk of deepening public cynicism and disaffection. This is one of the greatest dangers that public journalism faces. As Arthur Charity puts it, "Citizens will lose interest in journalism, too, if it does no better than politics in getting their judgment acted upon."[10]

Increasing Civic Engagement

Some newspapers have experimented with projects designed to give readers the opportunity to do more than just talk. In 1994, after several months of research, North Carolina's *Charlotte Observer* launched Taking Back Our Neighborhoods, a project that addressed the problem of rampant crime and violence in several of Charlotte's inner-city neighborhoods. The project included town meetings where neighborhood residents had the opportunity to have a dialogue with experts, elected officials, and representatives of government agencies. Eventually, the project mobilized the energies of hundreds of individuals and organizations and prompted action by city government that included tearing down dilapidated buildings and opening new parks and recreation facilities. The project can be criticized for having devoted too little attention to deliberation, instead proceeding directly to action, but by focusing on action it channeled the energies of citizens in the direction where they could have the greatest impact.

In 1993 the *Akron Beacon-Journal* followed up an extensive project on the state of race relations in that city with an initiative that gave readers the chance to get involved. The result has been an ongoing coalition of some 150 community organizations working to bring the races together, with the help of two community coordinators hired by the newspaper. Glenn Guzzo, managing editor of the newspaper, stressed that "the newspaper didn't set or drive the agenda; it merely worked as a catalyst to bring citizens together, then to report on whatever efforts took place in the community."[11]

Underlying this activist approach to public journalism is a more robust notion of the role of the citizen in a democracy. This vision of active citizenship is less concerned with participation in the electoral process than it is in enabling citizens to become more effective participants in the shared institutions and locations within which they live their daily lives: their children's' schools, their neighborhood parks and libraries, and the streets of their neighborhoods.

The idea of a public can be defined in different ways, but in one sense of the term it is having a problem or set of problems in common that defines a group of individuals as a public. Journalism *with* the public is journalism that becomes a medium for a conversation about those problems and for a shared quest for solutions.

What Role for Journalists? What Role for Experts?

Peter Parisi argues that the emphasis on solutions at the local level fails to address larger questions of cause and responsibility. Parisi is concerned that "civic journalism, as presently practiced, disguises a strongly conservative, privatized, volunteerist orientation."[12]

Better, says Parisi, for journalists to acknowledge their role as "defining and informing moderators of the discussion of social values" and to use that power to address public issues in constructive ways. Journalists can produce a richer public discourse, Parisi suggests, by drawing on the views of experts, and asking questions such as: "What can we do about this? What answers have been proposed by experts now, by people in the past, or by other countries?" Citizens would have a secondary role in this discourse, their opinions being brought in to "ground and validate" the discussion.

Parisi's points are well-taken. When civic journalists allow the local community alone to define the agenda, they lose the larger view and critical perspective that experts can bring to the conversation. And when they invite the local community to "solve it ourselves," they risk foreclosing the possibility that the causes and solutions of local problem need to be understood and addressed on a larger scale. A problem such as local crime may be inextricably linked to national economic policy and global trade.

The solution cannot be an either/or proposition. A public journalism that consists primarily of a conversation between journalists and experts and that relegates citizens to a secondary role is not likely to engage a disaffected populace. And a public journalism that fails to raise the larger questions cannot, over the long run, produce meaningful answers. In *Who Will Tell The People*, veteran political reporter William Greider articulates a vision of a newspaper that tries to serve both roles:

> A responsible newspaper would try to bring people back into that governing arena or at least warn them in a timely manner when they are about to be abused by it. A responsible newspaper would learn how to teach and listen and agitate. It would invent new formats that provide a tangible context in which people can understand power and also speak to it. . . .

I imagine a newspaper that is both loyal and smart, that approaches daily reality from the perspective of its readers, then uses its new sophistication to examine power in their behalf. A newspaper with those qualities would not solve the democratic problem, but it could begin to rebuild the connective tissue that is missing.[13]

The Disappearance of Public Space

Informed public opinion requires more than taking in information—even from a variety of sources. It requires processing that information in conversation with others, weighing opposing views, and in the process, discovering one's own opinion. One obstacle to public participation that many citizens face is the disappearance of public space. Such traditional meeting places as the barber shop, the town square, the small town cafe, "Main Street," the public library, the "Y," and the neighborhood tavern have been replaced, to greater or lesser degree, by institutions whose social (and in some cases legal) character is far more private (or in any case less social): the mall, the hair salon, the fast food restaurant, the video rental store, the health club, and the sports bar. This trend has created a need for news media to establish new forms of public space.

Rob Anderson, Robert Dardenne, and George Killenberg, authors of *The Conversation of Journalism*, argue that "The primary role of journalism in our view, and the only way by which it can survive as a viable institution in the public arena, is to take the responsibility to stimulate public dialogue on issues of common concern to a democratic public."[14] That is certainly an important function, but it is hardly the only way in which newspapers can contribute to the vitality of public life. The newspaper can also help to create or recreate public space, as many newspaper have already begun to do, by increasing the visibility it gives to community meetings and events, by organizing public meetings and forums on issues that are not otherwise being effectively addressed, and by making more of its news and editorial columns into public space where dialogue can take place.

For journalism to be a participatory medium does not require that newspapers engage every citizen or every reader in public deliberation or that they print every letter of every reader who wishes to express an opinion. Public deliberation may be an important part of participatory democracy, but newspapers also serve democracy simply by making visible the culture and daily life of the community they serve.

Although much of the debate about journalism ethics has focused on hard news reporting, feature and sports sections also have ethical significance, especially in terms of the values of public journalism. Traditionally, the feature sections, heirs to the women's pages and society pages, have been the one place in the newspaper devoted to the lives and interests of ordinary citizens—though seldom without biases regarding race, class, and gender. At some newspapers, the tendency is increasingly to fill these pages with content that addresses readers only as consumers—either as consumers of popular culture or as consumers of fashion, housewares, and home electronics. These sections, filled with stories about the same stars, movies, and new computer programs, become increasingly interchangeable from city to city. What is diminished in the process is the sense of connection to a place that the newspaper can create when it devotes its resources to telling stories about its own community.

As newspaper managements have adopted an explicitly or implicitly market-driven orientation, they have focused on making the newspaper a useful tool for readers as consumers. The public journalist's goal should be to make the newspaper, and especially the editorial and opinion pages, a tool for readers as citizens and members of communities. Defining a newspaper as a tool, rather than as an information medium implies a deeper kind of relationship. The information function is fulfilled when the reader learns something. The tool function is fulfilled when the reader does something. This can be writing a letter, joining an organization, registering to vote, attending a school board meeting, calling a legislator, or participating in a conversation with a neighbor.

Another impediment to public participation is a lack of role models. News reports on social trends routinely refer to the public as consumers, rather than as citizens. Many citizens are no doubt reluctant to participate in public life because they do not know how it is done or because their conception of politics has been shaped by the news media's emphasis on scandal and horse-race coverage. The news media can model and valorize citizen participation in a variety of ways. This is obviously a high institutional priority for the radio service of the Canadian Broadcasting Corporation (CBC), which serves a multicultural society deeply divided along ethnic lines. Relatively little of the CBC's news programming is devoted to "straight" news; a high proportion consists of talk shows on which guests and moderators model public debate and civilized disagreement.

Beyond Newspapers

What hope is there that a truly public journalism will thrive in the increasingly market-driven environment of the daily newspaper? Most public journalism has to this point been project-centered, rather than being incorporated into the daily routines of the newsroom. Open-ended public listening can be extremely labor-intensive and is a far less efficient way of gathering content to fill the news columns than following the traditional routines. Moreover, there is an inherent conflict between public journalism's emphasis on hearing the voice of the entire community and the market-driven newspaper's focus on attracting and serving the most demographically attractive segments of the market. Greider is not sanguine about the likelihood that newspapers will take seriously their democratic responsibilities:

> To embrace civic obligations that would alter the basic character of journalism might destabilize segments of the mass audience that media assemble for advertisers, the foundation of their commercial existence. Their readerships are already shrinking and news enterprises are not likely to invite more drastic losses by experimenting with their neutral political posture.[15]

It may be necessary to look beyond the urban daily newspaper for the survival of journalism. Most urban news media have long since abandoned anything beyond the most superficial coverage of local government. A few decades ago, you could expect any decent big city daily to provide in-depth coverage of city hall and other local branches of government. Today, the big city daily has become a big metropolitan daily, with a coverage area that may take in literally hundreds of branches of local government. Unless the actions of any one branch rise to the level of scandal, they cannot be covered consistently. But the abandonment of public affairs journalism by the news industry may create an opening for new forms of journalism based on partnerships between journalists and citizens. In many communities, the best source of information about what is happening at city hall or the school board is no longer the big metropolitan daily with its staff of journalism professionals, but the neighborhood and community press, which often relies on a collaboration between citizens and professional journalists.

Citizens who are not professional journalists now have, thanks to new technological developments, an unprecedented potential to become, themselves, mass communicators. Video cameras make it possible for citizen-journalists to document conditions in their neighborhoods or to circulate information about conditions half-way around the world. Cable television companies are now required to make local access channels available to the community, giving citizen journalists at least the technological means of reaching a mass audience. Desktop publishing software and home computers enable the ordinary citizen to publish flyers, newsletters, and handbills of a kind that a decade ago were beyond the reach of nonprofessionals. Computer-based bulletin boards function as electronic salons that are accessible to anyone with a computer and a modem.

Although many journalists may resist the idea of abandoning their traditional detachment, the reality is that if journalists want to continue to practice journalism, they face a struggle and need to find allies and to build alliances with that portion of the public that still cares about journalism. This must start with abandoning the contempt that many journalists express for the public and the humble recognition that journalists need the public even more than the public needs them.

Notes

Introduction

1. Speech given at the University of South Dakota, Vermillion, SD, Wednesday, October 16, 1996.

2. Jane McCartney, "News Lite," *American Journalism Record* (June 1997), p. 19.

3. Carl Sessions Stepp, "The Thrill Is Gone," *American Journalism Review* (October 1995), pp. 15–19.

4. Times Mirror Center for the People and the Press, Washington, DC, April 6, 1995, pp. 9, 29, cited in Jay Rosen, *Getting the Connections Right: Public Journalism and the Troubles in the Press* (New York: Twentieth Century Fund Press, 1996) p. 19.

5. Hoag Levins, "Newspapers May Lose 14% to Internet/Research Firm Predicts 5 Year Readership Decline," *E&P Interactive*, Friday, November 1, 1996.

6. Pew Research Center for The People and The Press, National Social Trust Survey, February 1997 (Washington, DC). Results summarized in the Pew Research Center's on-line *1997 Media Report*.

7. James Fallows, *Breaking the News: How the Media Undermine American Democracy* (New York: Pantheon Books, 1996), p. 3.

8. Jay Rosen and Davis Merritt Jr., "Public Journalism: Theory and Practice," an Occasional Paper of the Kettering Foundation (Dayton, OH: Kettering Foundation, 1994), p. 4.

9. Jay Black, Bob Steele, and Ralph Barney, *Doing Ethics in Journalism: A Handbook with Case Studies* (Greencastle, IN: The Sigma Delta Chi Foundation and the Society of Professional Journalists, 1993).

10. Ellen Hume, "Why the Press Blew the S&L Scandal," *New York Times*, May 24, 1990, A25; cited in Robert Parry, *Fooling America* (New York: William Morris, 1992), p. 12.

Chapter One

1. The National News Council, *After "Jimmy's World": Tightening Up in Editing* (New York: The National News Council, 1981).

2. Jay Black, "Journalism Ethics Education Since Janet Cooke," paper presented at the Poynter Institute, St. Petersburg, FL, 1991.

3. Stephen Klaidman and Tom L. Beauchamp, *The Virtuous Journalist* (New York: Oxford University Press, 1987).

4. Klaidman and Beauchamp, *The Virtuous Journalist*, p. 173.

5. Edmund B. Lambeth, *Committed Journalism: An Ethic for the Profession* (Bloomington: Indiana University Press, 1986), p. 29.

6. Jonathan Kwitny, "The Ethics of Ownership," paper presented at the Poynter Institute, St. Petersburg, FL, 1991, p. 1.

7. Kwitny, "The Ethics of Ownership," p. 1.

8. Lauren Millette, "Leap from News to Nude Falls Short," in *Solutions Today for Ethics Problems Tomorrow*, a special report by the ethics committee of the Society of Professional Journalists (Chicago: Society of Professional Journalists, 1989), pp. 4–5.

9. Ibid., p. 5.

10. Jim Mann, "Donna Rice Visit Triggers Controversy," in *Solutions Today*, p. 4.

11. Julian Sher, "Intruding on Private Pain: Emotional TV Segment Offers Hard Choice," *Fine Line, The Newsletter on Journalism Ethics* 1, no. 10 (January 1990), p. 2.

12. John Gillespie, "Do I Stop Him? Reporter's Arresting Question Is News," *Fine Line, The Newsletter on Journalism Ethics* 1, no. 10 (January 1990), p. 3.

13. Scott Libin and Jay Black, "Media Feeding Frenzy and the Abducted/Abused/Amnesiac Runaway: A Journalism Ethics Case Study," Poynter Online, February, 23, 1996 at http://www.poynter.org/research/me/me_cheryl.htm

14. Ibid.

15. Ibid.

16. Ibid.

17. Bob Steele, "The *Post*, the *Times*, and the Unabomber," Poynter Online, August 8, 1995, at http://www.poynter.org/research/me/me_una2htm.

18. Ibid.

19. John C. Merrill and Ralph D. Barney, eds., *Ethics and the Press* (New York: Hastings House, 1975).

20. Ben Johnson, "The Problem of Collecting and Presenting Information," in *Solutions Today*, p. 2.

21. Alasdair McIntyre, *After Virtue* (Notre Dame: University of Notre Dame Press, 1981).

22. James Carey, "Journalists Just Leave: The Ethics of an Anomalous Profession," in *Ethics and the Media*, Maile-Gene Jean Sagen, ed. (Iowa City: Iowa Humanities Board, 1987), pp. 5–19.

23. Gaye Tuchman, "Objectivity as Strategic Ritual: An Examination of Newsmen's Notions of Objectivity," *American Journal of Sociology* 77, no. 4 (January 1972), pp. 660–679.

24. Carey, "Journalists Just Leave," p. 6.

25. Duchesne Paul Drew, Maura Lerner, and Joe Rigert, "An Important Message for Guild Members," *Minneapolis–St. Paul Star Tribune*, April 29, 1996.

26. Mike Meyers, economics writer, *Minneapolis–St. Paul Star Tribune*, personal correspondence, July 19, 1997.

27. Cited in Margaret Carlisle Duncan, "Gender Bias in Televised Sports," *Extra!* (March/April 1991), p. 10.

Chapter Two

1. Steve Geimann, personal correspondence, August 3, 1997.

2. James Fallows, *Breaking the News: How the Media Undermine American Democracy* (New York: Pantheon Books, 1996), p. 83.

3. Ibid., p. 8.

4. Robert Parry, *Fooling America: How Washington Insiders Twist the Truth and Manufacture the Conventional Wisdom* (New York: William Morrow and Company, Inc., 1992,) p. 17.

5. Martin A. Lee and Norman Solomon, *Unreliable Sources: A Guide to Detecting Bias in News Media* (New York: Lyle Stuart, 1990).

6. Cited by Mark Hertsgaard in "Washington's Court Press," an article he wrote for *Nation*, June 10, 1996.

7. Jay Black, Bob Steele, and Ralph Barney, *Doing Ethics in Journalism: A Handbook with Case Studies* (Greencastle, IN: The Sigma Delta Chi Foundation and the Society of Professional Journalists, 1993), p. 20.

8. Alicia C. Shepard, "Moving Against Speaking Fees," *American Journalism Review* (November 1996), p. 15.

9. The newest version is reprinted in full in Debra Gersh Hernandez and Bill Schmitt, "SPJ Approves Ethics Code," *Editor and Publisher* (October 19, 1996).

10. Society of Professional Journalists Ethics Committee, Code of Ethics (Chicago: Society of Professional Journalists, 1996).

11. Edmund B. Lambeth, *Committed Journalism: An Ethic for the Profession* (Bloomington: Indiana University Press, 1986), p. 29.

12. Christopher Lasch, "Journalism, Publicity and the Lost Art of Argument," *Gannett Center Journal* (Spring 1990), p. 7.

13. John L. Hulteng, *Playing It Straight* (Chester, CT: Globe Pequot Press, 1981), offers an ASNE-authorized commentary on the Statement of Principles.

14. *Chicago Sun Times* Code of Professional Standards, October 1, 1974, reprinted in William L. Rivers, Wilbur Schramm, and Clifford G. Christians, *Responsibility in Mass Communications*, 3rd ed. (New York: Harper and Row, 1980), p. 294.

15. *Washington Post* Standards and Ethics, November 1977, reprinted in Rivers, Schramm, and Christians, *Responsibility in Mass Communications*, 3rd ed., p. 297.

16. Cited in Rivers, Schramm, and Christians, *Responsibility in Mass Communications*, 3rd ed., pp. 294–300.

17. Ibid., pp. 298–299.

18. Ibid., p. 295.

19. Society of Professional Journalists Code of Ethics, reprinted in full in Debra Gersh Hernandez and Bill Schmitt, "SPJ Approves Ethics Code," *Editor and Publisher* (October 19, 1996), quote from p. 51.

20. William Powers, "Getting Kathie Lee," *The New Republic*, June 9, 1997, p. 11.

21. Rivers, Schramm, and Christians, *Responsibility in Mass Communications*, p. 30.

22. Commission on Freedom of the Press, *A Free and Responsible Press* (Chicago: The University of Chicago Press, 1947).

23. Philip Meyer, *Ethical Journalism* (New York: Longman, 1987).

24. Cited in the 1981 Ethics Report of the Society of Professional Journalists.

25. Dorothy Smith, *The Everyday World as Problematic: A Feminist Sociology* (Boston: Northeastern University Press, 1987).

26. Manuel Galvan, "For Journalists, Inescapable Impact of Ethics," in *Solutions Today for Ethics Problems Tomorrow*, Manuel Galvan, ed. (Chicago: Society of Professional Journalists, 1989), p. 2.

Chapter Three

1. See, for example, Frank Luther Mott, *American Journalism: A History, 1690–1960* (New York: Macmillan, 1962).

2. W. Lance Bennett, *News: The Politics of Illusion*, 2nd. ed. (New York: Longman, 1988), p. 123.

3. Hazel Dicken-Garcia, *Journalistic Standards in Nineteenth-Century America* (Madison: University of Wisconsin Press, 1989), p. 8.

4. Dicken-Garcia, *Journalistic Standards*, p. 99.

5. Ibid., p. 99.

6. Michael Schudson, *Discovering the News* (New York: Basic Books, 1978), p. 20.

7. Ibid., p. 21.

8. J. Herbert Altschull, *Agents of Power* (New York: Longman, 1984), p. 63.

9. Dicken-Garcia, *Journalistic Standards*, p. 203.

10. Schudson, *Discovering the News*, p. 114.

11. Ibid., p. 112.

12. Joseph Pulitzer, "The College of Journalism," *North American Review*, 178 (1904), p. 657, cited in Schudson, *Discovering the News*, p. 153.

13. James Carey, "Journalists Just Leave: The Ethics of an Anomalous Profession." In *Ethics and the Media*, Maile-Gene Sagen, ed. (Iowa City: Iowa Humanities Board, 1987), p. 12.

14. Upton Sinclair, *The Brass Check: A Study of American Journalism* (Pasadena, CA: Upton Sinclair, 1920; reprint edition, New York: Arno, 1970).

15. Walter Lippmann, *Public Opinion*, p. 256, quoted in Schudson, *Discovering the News*, p. 151.

16. Walter Lippmann, *Liberty and the News*, p. 67, cited in Schudson, *Discovering the News*, p. 214.

17. Cited in Noam Chomsky, *Necessary Illusions* (Boston: South End Press, 1989), pp. 16–17.

18. Christopher Lasch, "Journalism, Publicity, and the Lost Art of Argument," *Gannett Center Journal* (Spring 1990), p. 7.

19. Quoted in "Some Problems in the Sociology of the Professions," *Daedalus* 92 (Fall 1963), pp. 669–688, cited in *Ethical Issues in Professional Life*, Joan C. Callahan, ed. (New York: Oxford University Press, 1988), p. 36.

20. John C. Merrill, *The Imperative of Freedom* (New York: Hastings House, 1974) pp. 133–42, cited in Callahan, *Ethical Issues in Professional Life*, pp. 40–41.

21. Schudson, *Discovering the News*, p. 155.

22. Herbert J. Gans, *Deciding What's News* (New York: Vintage, 1979), p. 184.

23. Cited in Altschull, *Agents of Power*, p. 180.

24. Cited in William L. Rivers, Wilbur Schramm, and Clifford G. Christians, *Responsibility in Mass Communications*, 3rd ed. (New York: Harper & Row, 1980), p. 43.

25. Richard Strout, *The Christian Science Monitor*, May 27, 1950, cited in Edwin R. Bayley, *Joe McCarthy and the Press* (New York: Pantheon Books, 1982), p. 75.

26. Paul H. Weaver, "The New Journalism and the Old," reprinted in *Ethics and the Press*, John C. Merrill and Ralph D. Barney, eds. (New York: Hastings House, 1975), p. 90.

27. John L. Hulteng, *Playing It Straight* (Chester, CT: Globe Pequot Press, 1981), p. 46.

28. National News Council, *After "Jimmy's World": Tightening Up in Editing* (Washington, DC: The National News Council, 1981), p. 3.

29. Cited in Mercedes L. de Uriarte, "'Jimmy's World': Black Void in a White Press," paper delivered at the Poynter Institute, St. Petersburg, FL, 1991, p. 7.

30. See Theodore L. Glasser, "Professionalism and the Derision of Diversity: The Case of the Education of Journalists," *The Journal of Communication* 42, no. 2 (Spring 1992), pp. 131–140.

31. David Eason, "On Journalistic Authority: The Janet Cooke Scandal," *Critical Studies in Mass Communications* (December 1986), p. 434.

32. "Capital Offense," *The Wall Street Journal*, April 17, p. 1, cited in Eason, *On Journalistic Authority*, p. 432.

Chpater Four

1. Claude-Jean Bertrand, in Clifford G. Christians, John P. Ferre, and P. Mark Fackler, *Good News: Social Ethics and the Press* (New York: Oxford University Press, 1993), p. viii.

2. Doug Underwood, *When MBAs Rule the Newsroom* (New York: Columbia University Press, 1993), p. 74.

3. Hanno Hardt, "The End of Journalism: Media and Newsworkers in the United States," *Javnost/The Public Journal of the European Institute for Communication and Culture* 3, no. 3 (1996), p. 33.

4. Cited in Marty Linsky, "Reporters and Angst: The View from the Top," *The Poynter Report* (Spring 1997), p. 9.

5. Gene Roberts, "The Local Press Is a Tragedy Waiting to Happen," *The Washington Spectator* 22, no. 13 (July 1996), p 1.

6. Ibid., p 2.

7. Ibid., pp. 1–2.

8. Robert H. Giles, "Change Shapes Trends in Newspaper Management," *Newspaper Research Journal* 14, no. 2 (Spring 1993), pp. 32–39.

9. Carol Bradley Shirley, "Where Have You Been?" *Columbia Journalism Review* 31, no. 2 (July/August 1992), pp. 25–26, cited in Clifford G. Christians, Mark Fackler, and Kim B. Rotzoll, *Media Ethics: Cases & Moral Reasoning*, 4th ed. (White Plains, NY: Longmans, 1995), p. 48.

10. Roberts, "The Local Press Is a Tragedy Waiting to Happen," p. 3.

11. Alison Carper, "Paint-by-Numbers Journalism: How Reader Surveys and Focus Groups Subvert a Democratic Press," Discussion Paper D-19, April 1995, p. 9. Joan Shorenstein Center for Press, Politics, and Public Policy, Harvard University.

12. As reported on Bill Moyers' series, *The Public Mind*, broadcast on PBS November 1989. The segment, "Illusions of News," was produced by Alvin H. Perlmutter, Inc., and Public Affairs Television, Inc. (Alexandria, VA: PBS Video, 1989).

13. Christopher Lasch, letter to Nina Easton, September 24, 1992; copy provided by the author.

14. Edward W. Jones, managing editor of the *Fredricksburg, Virginia, Free Lance-Star*, in Iver Peterson, "Editors Discuss Frustrations in Age of Refrigerator Magnet Journalism," *New York Times*, April 14, 1997, D9.

15. Hanno Hardt, "The End of Journalism," pp. 21–22.

16. Alan Wolfe, *Harpers*, October 1994.

17. David Leonhardt, "Two-Tier Marketing Companies Are Tailoring Their Products and Pitches to Two Different Americas," *Business Week*, March 17, 1997.

18. Colin Sparks, "Newspapers, the Internet and Democracy," *Javnost/The Public Journal of the European Institute for Communication and Culture* 3, no. 3 (1996), p. 47.

19. Ibid., p. 37.

20. Ibid., p. 38.

21. Philip Meyer, "Learning to Love Lower Profits," *American Journalism Review* (1995), p. 130.

Chapter Five

1. Fred D'Agostino, "Transcendence and Conversation: Two Conceptions of Objectivity," *American Philosophical Quarterly*, 30, no. 2 (April 1993), p. 87.

2. Everette E. Dennis, *Reshaping the Media* (Newbury Park, CA: Sage Publications, 1989), p. 83.

3. Walter Lippmann, *Liberty and the News* (New York: Harcourt Brace and Howe, 1920), p. 82. Cited in Michael Schudson, *Discovering the News* (New York: Basic Books, 1978) p. 152.

4. Gaye Tuchman, "Objectivity as Strategic Ritual: An Examination of Newsmen's Notions of Objectivity," *American Journal of Sociology* 77, no. 4 (January 1972), p. 660.

5. George Lardner Jr., cited in Lou Cannon, *Reporting: An Inside View* (Sacramento: California Journal Press, 1977), p. 44.

6. Cited in Robert H. Bremner, *From the Depths: The Discovery of Poverty in the United States* (New York: New York University Press, 1972), p. 140.

7. Ibid., p. 141.

8. Donald McDonald, "Is Objectivity Possible?" in *Ethics and the Press*, John C. Merrill and Ralph D. Barney, eds. (New York: Hastings House, 1975), p. 81.

9. Douglass Cater in *The Reporter*, June 6, 1950, cited in Edwin R. Bayley, *Joe McCarthy and the Press* (New York, Pantheon Books, 1982), p. 76.

10. Bayley, *Joe McCarthy and the Press*, p. 85.

11. Herbert Brucker, *Freedom of Information*, 1949, p. 206, cited in Cannon, *Reporting: An Inside View*, p. 36.

12. John Hulteng, *The News Media: What Makes Them Tick?* (Englewood Cliffs, NJ: Prentice-Hall, 1979) p. 94.

13. Philip Meyer, *Ethical Journalism* (New York: Longman, 1987) p. 47.

14. Ibid., p. 60.

15. Ibid., p. 47.

16. Cited in Cannon, *Reporting: An Inside View*, p. 36.

17. Stephen Klaidman and Tom L. Beauchamp, *The Virtuous Journalist* (New York: Oxford University Press, 1987), p. 70.

18. Ibid., p. 33.

19. Ibid., p. 33.

20. Herbert Gans, *Deciding What's News* (New York: Vintage Books, 1980), p. 42.

21. Klaidman and Beauchamp, *The Virtuous Journalist*, p. 44.

22. Cited in Cannon, *Reporting: An Inside View*, p. 35. Harwood goes on to ask, rhetorically, "Could we do a more representative picture? Yes." That is a conclusion he does not support.

23. Edward Herman and Noam Chomsky, *Manufacturing Consent: The Political Economy of the Mass Media* (New York: Pantheon Books, 1988), p. 24.

24. Lawrence Soley, *The News Shapers* (New York: Praeger, 1992), p. 19.

25. Cannon, *Reporting: An Inside View,* p. 44.

26. Mark Fishman, *Manufacturing the News* (Austin: University of Texas Press, 1980), p. 77.

27. Ibid., p. 77.

28. Gaye Tuchman, *Making News* (New York: The Free Press, 1978).

29. See Stanton Peele, *The Diseasing of America* (Lexington, MA: Lexington Books, 1990), and Herbert Fingarette, *Heavy Drinking: The Myth of Alcoholism as a Disease* (Berkeley: University of California Press, 1988).

30. Howard Kurtz, *Media Circus: The Trouble with America's Newspapers* (New York: Times Books, 1993), p. 41.

Chapter Six

1. Mark Fishman, *Manufacturing the News* (Austin: University of Texas Press, 1980), p. 45.

2. Ibid., p. 5

3. Ibid., p. 9.

4. Ibid., p. 10.

5. Daniel Boorstin, *The Image: A Guide to Pseudo-Events in America* (New York: Harper and Row, 1964), pp. 11–12, cited in William L. Rivers, Wilbur Schramm, and Clifford G. Christians, *Responsibility in Mass Communications* (New York: Harper & Row, 1980), p. 138.

6. Rivers, Schramm, and Christians, *Responsibility in Mass Communications,* p. 141.

7. John Pauly, "Foreword," in *The Conversation of Journalism: Communication, Community and News,* Rob Anderson, Robert Dardenne, and George M. Kellenberg, eds. (Westport, CT: Praeger, 1994), p. ix.

8. An excellent discussion of the social impact of the mass media can be found in Joshua Meyrowitz's *No Sense of Place: The Impact of Electronic Media on Social Behavior* (New York: Oxford University Press, 1985).

9. Cited in Schramm, Rivers, and Christians, *Responsibility in Mass Communications,* p. 289.

10. Cited in Debra Gersh Hernandez and Bill Schmitt, "SPJ Approves Ethics Code," *Editor and Publisher* (October 19, 1996), p. 22.

11. Elaine Rapping, *The Looking Glass World of Nonfiction Television* (Boston: South End Press, 1987), p. 6.

12. Michel Foucault, "Two Lectures," in *Power/Knowledge: Selected Interviews and Other Writings, 1972–1977* (New York: Pantheon Books, 1980), p. 93.

13. James Carey, "The Press and Public Discourse," *The Center Magazine* (March/April 1987).

14. Benedict Anderson, *Imagined Communities: Reflections on the Origin and Spread of Nationalism,* rev. ed. (London and New York: Verso Books, 1991).

15. Alvin Gouldner, *The Dialectic of Ideology and Technology* (New York: Oxford University Press, 1976), p. 96.

16. Rapping, *The Looking Glass World of Nonfiction Television,* p. 7.

17. Fishman, *Manufacturing the News,* p. 88.

18. Walter Lippmann, *Public Opinion* (New York: Harcourt, Brace & Co., 1922), p. 310.

19. John L. McKnight, "Regenerating Community," *Kettering Review* (Fall 1989), pp. 42–43.

20. See, for example, Robert D. Putnam's "Bowling Alone: America's Declining Social Capital," *Journal of Democracy* 6, no. 1 (January 1995), pp. 65–78.

21. McKnight, "Regenerating Community," pp. 40–50.

22. James Carey, "Journalists Just Leave: The Ethics of an Anomalous Profession," in *Ethics and the Media,* Maile-Gene Sagen, ed. (Iowa City: Iowa Humanities Board, 1987), p. 14.

23. Robert Entman, *Democracy Without Citizens: Media and the Decay of American Politics* (New York: Oxford University Press, 1989), pp. 125–126.

24. Claude Fischer, "Finding the 'Lost' Community: Facts and Fictions," *Tikkun* (November/December 1988), pp. 69–72.

25. Benjamin Barber, *Strong Democracy: Participatory Politics for a New Age* (Berkeley: University of California Press, 1984), pp. 93–94.

26. See, for example, Mary Ann Glendon, *Right Talk: The Impoverishment of Political Discourse* (New York: The Free Press, 1991).

27. Christopher Lasch, "Journalism, Publicity and the Lost Art of Argument," *Gannett Center Journal* (Spring 1990), p. 1.

28. Lasch, "Journalism, Publicity and the Lost Art of Argument," p. 1.

29. McKnight, "Regenerating Community," p. 42.

30. Ibid., p. 46.

31. James Fallows, *Breaking the News: How the Media Undermine American Democracy* (New York: Pantheon Books, 1996), p. 7.

32. Putnam, "Bowling Alone: America's Declining Social Capital," p. 68.

Chapter Seven

1. James Carey, "The Press and Public Discourse," *The Center Magazine* (March/April 1987), p. 14.

2. John Dewey, *The Public and Its Problems* (Athens: Ohio University Press, n.d.; originally published in 1927), p. 208.

3. Ibid., p. 142.

4. Juergen Habermas, *The Structural Transformation of the Public Sphere: An Inquiry into a Category of Bourgeois Society,* Thomas Burger, trans. (Cambridge, MA: MIT Press, 1991), pp. 184–185.

5. Benjamin Barber, *Strong Democracy: Participatory Politics for a New Age* (Berkeley: University of California Press, 1984), pp. 93–94.

6. Ibid., p. 97.

7. John B. Thompson, *Ideology and Modern Culture* (Stanford, CA: Stanford University Press, 1990), pp. 119–120.

8. Christopher Norris, *Uncritical Theory: Postmodernism, Intellectuals, and the Gulf War* (Amherst: University of Massachusetts Press, 1992).

9. C. S. Peirce, *Philosophical Writings of Peirce*, Justus Buchler, ed. (New York: Dover Books, 1955), p. 38, cited in John P. Murphy, *Pragmatism: From Peirce to Davidson* (Boulder: Westview Press, 1990), pp. 3–4.

Chapter Eight

1. Jay Rosen, posting to the on-line Civic Gang list-serv, July 16, 1997. This material will also appear in Rosen's chapter, "The Action of the Idea: Public Journalism in Built Form,"

in *The Idea of Public Journalism,* Theodore Glasser, ed. (New York: Guilford Press, forthcoming).

2. Peter Parisi, personal correspondence, May 17, 1997.

3. David Blomquist and Cliff Zukin, "Does Public Journalism Work?: The Campaign Central Experience." Report released by the Pew Center for Public Journalism, May 21, 1997.

4. Michael Kelly, "Media Culpa," *The New Yorker,* December 9, 1996, p. 6.

5. Daniel Yankelovich, "How Public Opinion Really Works," *Fortune* (October 5, 1992), pp. 102–108.

6. John Dewey, *The Public and Its Problems* (Athens: Ohio University Press, n.d.; originally published in 1927), p. 143.

7. Ibid., p. 147.

8. Ibid., p. 178.

9. Pew Charitable Trusts, Peggy Anderson, report writer, "Civic Lessons: Report on Four Civic Journalism Projects Funded by the Pew Center for Civic Journalism," The Pew Charitable Trusts, 1997, p. 13.

10. Arthur Charity, *Doing Public Journalism* (New York: Guilford Press, 1996), p. 125.

11. Glenn Guzzo, "Mirror of a Community," in *Public Journalism: What It Means, Who Is Practicing It, How It Is Done* (APME Readership Committee, 1994), p. 20.

12. Posting to the "Civic Gang" on-line mailing list April 30, 1997. These ideas are developed by Parisi at greater length in a forthcoming article, "Towards a 'Philosophy of Framing': New Narratives for Public Journalism," to appear in *Journalism and Mass Communication Quarterly* sometime in 1998.

13. William Greider, *Who Will Tell the People: The Betrayal of American Democracy* (New York: Touchstone Books/Simon & Schuster, 1992), pp. 304–305.

14. Rob Anderson, Robert Dardenne, and George M. Killenberg *The Conversation of Journalism: Communication, Community and News* (Westport, CT: Praeger, 1994).

15. Greider, *Who Will Tell the People,* p. 305.

Bibliography

Abrahamson, Jeffrey B. 1990. "Four Criticisms of Press Ethics." In *Democracy and the Mass Media*, Judith Lichtenberg, ed. New York: Cambridge University Press.

Altschull, J. Herbert. 1984. *Agents of Power.* New York: Longman.

American Press Institute. 1996. *The Printed Newspaper: Its Future and Its Role.* Collected comments from the J. Montgomery Curtis Memorial Seminar, September 24–26. Reston, VA: American Press Institute.

Anderson, Rob, Robert Dardenne, and George M. Killenberg. 1994. *The Conversation of Journalism: Communication, Community and News.* Westport, CT: Praeger.

Associated Press Managing Editors (APME) Readership Committee. 1994. *Public Journalism: What It Means, Who Is Practicing It, How It Is Done.* APME Report.

Bagdikian, Ben. 1987. *The Media Monopoly,* 2nd ed. Boston: Beacon Press.

Balough, Maggie. 1996. "Ethics Code Revision Set for Vote," *The Quill* 83, no. 6 (July 17).

Barber, Benjamin. 1984. *Strong Democracy: Participatory Politics for a New Age.* Berkeley: University of California Press.

Barsamian, David. 1992. *Stenographers to Power: Media and Propaganda.* Monroe, ME: Common Courage Press.

Bayley, Edwin R. 1982. *Joe McCarthy and the Press.* New York: Pantheon Books.

Bellah, Robert N., Richard Madsen, William M. Sullivan, Ann Swidler, and Steven M. Tipton. 1991. *The Good Society.* New York: Alfred A. Knopf.

Bennett, W. Lance. 1988. *News: The Politics of Illusion.* 2nd ed. New York: Longman.

Bernstein, Richard. 1982. *Beyond Objectivism and Relativism.* Philadelphia: University of Pennsylvania Press.

Black, Jay. 1991. "Journalism Ethics Education Since Janet Cooke." Paper presented at the Poynter Institute, St. Petersburg, FL.

_____. 1996. "Media Feeding Frenzy and the Abducted/Abused/Amnesiac/Runaway? A Journalism Ethics Case Study." The Poynter Institute, February 23.

Black, Jay, Bob Steele, and Ralph Barney. 1993. *Doing Ethics in Journalism: A Handbook with Case Studies.* Greencastle, IN: The Sigma Delta Chi Foundation and the Society of Professional Journalists.

Boorstin, Daniel. 1964. *The Image: A Guide to Pseudo-Events in America.* New York: Harper and Row.

Braaten, Jane. 1991. *Habermas's Critical Theory of Society.* Albany: State University of New York Press.

Bremner, Robert H. 1972. *From the Depths: The Discovery of Poverty in the United States.* New York: New York University Press.

Callahan, Joan C., ed. 1988. *Ethical Issues in Professional Life.* New York: Oxford University Press.

Cannon, Lou. 1977. *Reporting: An Inside View*. Sacramento: California Journal Press.

Carey, James. 1987a. "Journalists Just Leave: The Ethics of an Anomalous Profession." In *Ethics and the Media*, Maile-Gene Sagen, ed. Iowa City: Iowa Humanities Board.

_____. 1987b. "The Press and Public Discourse." *The Center Magazine* (March/April).

Carper, Alison. 1995. "Paint-by-Numbers Journalism: How Reader Surveys and Focus Groups Subvert a Democratic Press," Discussion Paper D-19, April. Joan Shorenstein Center for Press, Politics, and Public Policy, Harvard University.

Charity, Arthur. 1993. "What Readers Want: A Vote for a Very Different Model," *Columbia Journalism Review* 32, no. 4 (November/December).

_____. 1996. *Doing Public Journalism*. New York: Guilford Press.

Chomsky, Noam. 1989. *Necessary Illusions: Thought Control in Democratic Societies*. Boston: South End Press.

Christians, Clifford G., Mark Fackler, and Kim B. Rotzoll. 1995. *Media Ethics: Cases & Moral Reasoning*, 4th ed. White Plains, NY: Longmans.

Christians, Clifford G., John P. Ferre, and P. Mark Fackler. 1993. *Good News: Social Ethics and the Press*. New York: Oxford University Press.

Commission on Freedom of the Press. 1947. *A Free and Responsible Press*. Chicago: The University of Chicago Press.

Craft, Christine. 1988. *Too Old, Too Ugly, and Not Deferential to Men*. New York: Dell Publishing.

Cranberg, Gilbert. 1997. "Trimming the Fringe: How Newspapers Shun Low-Income Readers," *Columbia Journalism Review* 35, no. 1 (March/April).

D'Agostino, Fred. 1993. "Transcendence and Conversation: Two Conceptions of Objectivity." *American Philosophical Quarterly* 30, No. 2 (April).

D'Amico, Alfonso J. 1978. *Individuality and Community: The Social and Political Thought of John Dewey*. Gainesville: University Presses of Florida.

de Uriarte, Mercedes L. 1991. "'Jimmy's World': Black Void in a White Press." Paper delivered at the Poynter Institute, St. Petersburg, FL.

Dennis, Everette E. 1989. *Reshaping the Media*. Newbury Park, CA: Sage Publications.

Dewey, John. n.d.; originally published in 1927. *The Public and Its Problems*. Athens: Ohio University Press.

Dicken-Garcia, Hazel. 1989. *Journalistic Standards in Nineteenth-Century America*. Madison: University of Wisconsin Press.

Duncan, Margaret Carlisle. 1991. "Gender Bias in Televised Sports," *Extra!* (March/April).

Eason, David. 1986. "On Journalistic Authority: The Janet Cooke Scandal," *Critical Studies in Mass Communications* 3 (December).

Ellul, Jacques. 1973. *Propaganda*. New York: Vintage Books.

Emery, Michael, and Edwin Emery. 1992. *The Press and America: An Interpretive History of the Mass Media*, 7th ed. Englewood Cliffs, NJ: Prentice Hall.

Entman, Robert. 1989. *Democracy Without Citizens: Media and the Decay of American Politics*. New York: Oxford University Press.

Fallows, James. 1996. *Breaking the News: How the Media Undermine American Democracy*. New York: Pantheon Books.

Ferguson, Marilyn. 1984. *The Feminist Case Against Bureaucracy*. Philadelphia: Temple University Press.

Fibich, Linda. 1995. "Under Siege," *American Journalism Review* (September).

Fingarette, Herbert. 1988. *Heavy Drinking: The Myth of Alcoholism as a Disease.* Berkeley: University of California Press.

Fischer, Claude. 1988. "Finding the 'Lost' Community: Facts and Fictions," *Tikkun* (November/December).

Fishman, Mark. 1980. *Manufacturing the News.* Austin, University of Texas Press.

Foucault, Michel. 1980. *Power/Knowledge: Selected Interviews and Other Writings, 1972–1977.* New York: Pantheon Books.

Funkhouser, G. Ray, and Eugene F. Shaw. 1990. "How Synthetic Experience Shapes Social Reality," *Journal of Communication* (Spring).

Galvan, Manuel. 1989. "For Journalists, Inescapable Impact of Ethics." In *Solutions Today for Ethics Problems Tomorrow,* Manuel Galvan, ed. Chicago: Society of Professional Journalists.

Galvan, Manuel, ed. 1989. *Solutions Today for Ethics Problems Tomorrow.* Chicago: Society of Professional Journalists.

Gans, Herbert. 1979. *Deciding What's News.* New York: Vintage Books.

Gilmore, Gene, and Robert Root. 1978. "Ethics for Newsmen." In *Ethics and the Press,* John C. Merrill and Ralph D. Barney, eds. New York: Hastings House.

Gitlin, Todd. 1980. *The Whole World Is Watching.* Berkeley: University of California Press.

Glasser, Theodore L. 1984. "Objectivity Precludes Responsibility," *The Quill* (May).

_____. 1992. "Professionalism and the Derision of Diversity: The Case of the Education of Journalists," *The Journal of Communication* 42, no. 2 (Spring).

Glendon, Mary Ann. 1991. *Right Talk: The Impoverishment of Political Discourse.* New York: The Free Press.

Goldstein, Tom. 1985. *The News at Any Cost: How Journalists Compromise Their Ethics to Shape the News.* New York: Simon and Schuster.

Gouldner, Alvin. 1976. *The Dialectic of Ideology and Technology.* New York: Oxford University Press.

Greider, William. 1992. *Who Will Tell the People: The Betrayal of American Democracy.* New York: Touchstone Books/Simon & Schuster.

Gunn, Giles. 1992. *Thinking Across the American Grain: Ideology, Intellect, and the New Pragmatism.* Chicago: The University of Chicago Press.

Guzzo, Glenn. 1994. "Mirror of a Community," in *Public Journalism: What It Means, Who Is Practicing It, How It Is Done.* Associated Press Managing Editors (APME) Readership Committee.

Habermas, Juergen. 1991. *The Structural Transformation of the Public Sphere: An Inquiry into a Category of Bourgeois Society.* Thomas Burger, trans. Cambridge, MA: MIT Press.

Hardt, Hanno. 1996. "The End of Journalism: Media and Newsworkers in the United States," *Javnost/The Public Journal of the European Institute for Communication and Culture* 3, no. 3.

Harwood, Richard. 1997. "Reporting in The Absence of News," *The Washington Post,* Monday, April 28, p. A19.

Herman, Edward, and Noam Chomsky. 1988. *Manufacturing Consent: The Political Economy of the Mass Media.* New York: Pantheon Books.

Hernandez, Debra Gersh, and Bill Schmitt. 1996. "SPJ Approves Ethics Code," *Editor and Publisher* (October 19).

Hertsgaard, Mark. 1996. "Washington's Court Press," *Nation,* June 10.

Hulteng, John L. 1979. *The News Media: What Makes Them Tick?* Englewood Cliffs, NJ: Prentice-Hall.

_____. 1981. *Playing It Straight.* Chester, CT: Globe Pequot Press.

Johnson, Ben. 1989. "The Problem of Collecting and Presenting Information." In *Solutions Today for Ethics Problems Tomorrow,* Manuel Galvan, ed. Chicago: Society of Professional Journalists.

Katz, Jon. 1992. "Rock, Rap and Movies Bring You the News," *Rolling Stone* (March 5).

Kellner, Douglas. 1990. *Television and the Crisis of Democracy.* Boulder: Westview Press.

_____. 1992. *The Persian Gulf TV War.* Boulder: Westview Press.

Klaidman, Stephen, and Tom L. Beauchamp. 1987. *The Virtuous Journalist.* New York: Oxford University Press.

Kurtz, Howard. 1993. *Media Circus: The Trouble with America's Newspapers.* New York: Times Books.

Kwitny, Jonathan. 1991. "The Ethics of Ownership." Paper presented at the Poynter Institute, St. Petersburg, FL.

Lambeth, Edmund B. 1986. *Committed Journalism: An Ethic for the Profession.* Bloomington: Indiana University Press.

Lasch, Christopher. 1990a. "Stop Making Sense," *NEWSINC.* (December).

_____. 1990b. "Journalism, Publicity and the Lost Art of Argument," *Gannett Center Journal* (Spring).

Lee, Martin A., and Norman Solomon. 1990. *Unreliable Sources: A Guide to Detecting Bias in News Media.* New York: Lyle Stuart.

Levins, Hoag. 1996. "Newspapers May Lose 14% to Internet/Research Firm Predicts 5 Year Readership Decline," *E&P Interactive* (Friday, November 1).

Linsky, Marty. 1997. "Reporters and Angst: The View from the Top," Poynter Report.

Lippmann, Walter. 1920. *Liberty and the News.* New York: Harcourt Brace and Howe.

_____. 1922. *Public Opinion.* New York: Harcourt Brace & Co.

MacDonnell, Diane. 1986. *Theories of Discourse.* London: Basil Blackwell.

Mankiewicz, Frank, and Joel Swerdlow. 1978. *Remote Control: Television and the Manipulation of American Life.* New York: Ballantine Books.

Manoff, Robert Karl, and Michael Schudson, eds. 1987. *Reading the News.* New York: Pantheon Books.

McCartney, James. 1997. "News Lite," *American Journalism Review* 19, no. 5 (June).

McCulloch, Frank, ed. 1984. *Drawing the Line: How 31 Editors Solved Their Toughest Ethical Dilemmas.* Washington, DC: American Society of Newspaper Editors.

McDonald, Donald. 1975. "Is Objectivity Possible?" In *Ethics and the Press,* John C. Merrill and Ralph D. Barney, eds. New York: Hastings House.

McIntyre, Alasdair. 1981. *After Virtue.* Notre Dame: University of Notre Dame Press.

McKnight, John L. 1989. "Regenerating Community," *Kettering Review* (Fall).

Merrill, John C., and Ralph D. Barney, eds. 1975. *Ethics and the Press.* New York: Hastings House.

Meyer, Philip. 1987. *Ethical Journalism.* New York: Longman.

_____. 1996. "Learning to Love Lower Profits," *American Journalism Review.*

Meyrowitz, Joshua. 1985. *No Sense of Place: The Impact of Electronic Media on Social Behavior.* New York: Oxford University Press.

Mott, Frank Luther. 1962. *American Journalism: A History, 1690–1960.* New York: Macmillan.

Murphy, John P. 1990. *Pragmatism: From Peirce to Davidson.* Boulder: Westview Press.

National News Council. 1981. *After "Jimmy's World": Tightening Up in Editing.* New York: The National News Council.

Norris, Christopher. 1992. *Uncritical Theory: Postmodernism, Intellectuals, and the Gulf War.* Amherst: University of Massachusetts Press.

Parenti, Michael. 1986. *Inventing Reality: The Politics of the Mass Media.* New York: St. Martin's Press.

Parisi, Peter. Forthcoming. "Toward a 'Philosophy of Framing': News Narratives for Public Journalism," *Journalism and Mass Communication Quarterly.*

Parker, Elliott. 1996. "'Market-driven' Business and Demands on Journalists." Paper given at the 1996 Conference of the Association of Educators in Journalism and Mass Communications.

Parry, Robert. 1992. *Fooling America: How Washington Insiders Twist the Truth and Manufacture the Conventional Wisdom.* New York: William Morrow and Company, Inc.

Pauly, John. 1994. "Foreword," for *The Conversation of Journalism: Communication, Community, and News,* Rob Anderson, Robert Dardenne, and George M. Kellenberg, eds. Westport, CT: Praeger.

Peele, Stanton. 1990. *The Diseasing of America.* Lexington, MA: Lexington Books.

Peirce, C. S. 1955. *Philosophical Writings of Peirce.* Justus Buchler, ed. New York: Dover Books.

Peterson, Iver. 1997. "Editors Discuss Frustrations in Age of Refrigerator Magnet Journalism," *New York Times.*

Pew Charitable Trusts (Peggy Anderson, report writer). 1997. "Civic Lessons: Report on Four Civic Journalism Projects Funded by the Pew Center for Civic Journalism." Philadelphia: The Pew Charitable Trusts.

Postman, Neil. 1986. *Amusing Ourselves to Death.* New York: Penguin Books.

Powers, William. 1996. "The Local Press Is a Tragedy Waiting to Happen," *The Washington Spectator* 22, no. 13 (July 1).

Putnam, Robert D. 1995. "Bowling Alone: America's Declining Social Capital," *Journal of Democracy* 6, no. 1 (January).

_____. 1996. "The Strange Disappearance of Civic America," *The American Prospect* (Winter).

Rapping, Elaine. 1987. *The Looking Glass World of Nonfiction Television.* Boston: South End Press.

Rivers, William L., Wilbur Schramm, and Clifford G. Christians. 1980. *Responsibility in Mass Communications,* 3rd ed. New York: Harper & Row.

Roberts, Gene. 1996a. "Drowning in Shallow Water," *Columbia Journalism Review* 35, no. 1 (May/June).

_____. 1996b. "The Local Press Is a Tragedy Waiting to Happen," *The Washington Spectator* 22, no. 13 (July 1).

Rorty, Richard. 1991. *Objectivity, Relativism and Truth: Philosophical Papers, Volume 1.* Cambridge, UK: Cambridge University Press.

Rosen, Jay. 1991. "Making Journalism More Public," *Communication* 12.

_____. 1992a. "No Content: The Press, Politics, and Public Philosophy," *Tikkun* 7, no. 3 (May/June).

_____. 1992b. "Rituals of Contempt: On a Dangerous Tendency in American Journalism," *Culturefront* 1, no. 2 (September).

_____. 1993. "Beyond Objectivity," *Nieman Reports* (Winter).

_____. 1996. *Getting the Connections Right: Public Journalism and the Troubles in the Press.* New York: Twentieth Century Fund Press.

Rucinski, Dianne. 1991. "The Centrality of Reciprocity to Communication and Democracy," *Critical Studies in Communication* 8 (June).

Sagen, Maile-Gene. 1987. *Ethics and the Media* (Iowa City: Iowa Humanities Board, 1987)

Said, Edward. 1981. *Covering Islam.* New York: Pantheon Books.

Schiller, Dan. 1981. *Objectivity and the News.* Philadelphia: University of Pennsylvania Press.

Schiller, Herbert. 1973. *The Mind Managers.* Boston: Beacon Press.

Schudson, Michael. 1978. *Discovering the News.* New York: Basic Books.

Schwartz, Tony. 1981. *Media: The Second God.* New York: Random House.

Shepard, Alicia C. 1996. "Moving Against Speaking Fees," *American Journalism Review* (November).

Sinclair, Upton. 1920 *The Brass Check: A Study of American Journalism.* Pasadena, CA: Upton Sinclair. Reprint edition, New York: Arno, 1970.

Smith, Dorothy. 1987. *The Everyday World as Problematic: A Feminist Sociology.* Boston: Northeastern University Press.

Soley, Lawrence. 1992. *The News Shapers.* New York: Praeger.

Sparks, Colin. 1996. "Newspapers, the Internet and Democracy," *Javnost/The Public Journal of the European Institute for Communication and Culture* 3, no. 3.

Stepp, Carl Sessions. 1995. "The Thrill Is Gone," *American Journalism Review* (November/December).

_____. 1995. *American Journalism Review* (October).

Thompson, John B. 1990. *Ideology and Modern Culture.* Stanford, CA: Stanford University Press.

Tuchman, Gaye. 1972. "Objectivity as Strategic Ritual: An Examination of Newsmen's Notions of Objectivity," *American Journal of Sociology,* 77, no. 4 (January).

_____. 1978. *Making News.* New York: The Free Press.

Underwood, Doug. 1993. *When MBAs Rule the Newsroom.* New York: Columbia University Press.

Vanocur, Sander. 1980. "TV's Failed Promise." In *Ethics, Morality and the Media,* Lee Thayer, ed. New York: Hastings House.

Yankelovich, Daniel. 1992. "How Public Opinion Really Works," *Fortune* (October 5), pp. 102–108.

Index